LED

# THE
# EARTHQUAKE
## HANDBOOK

# THE EARTH

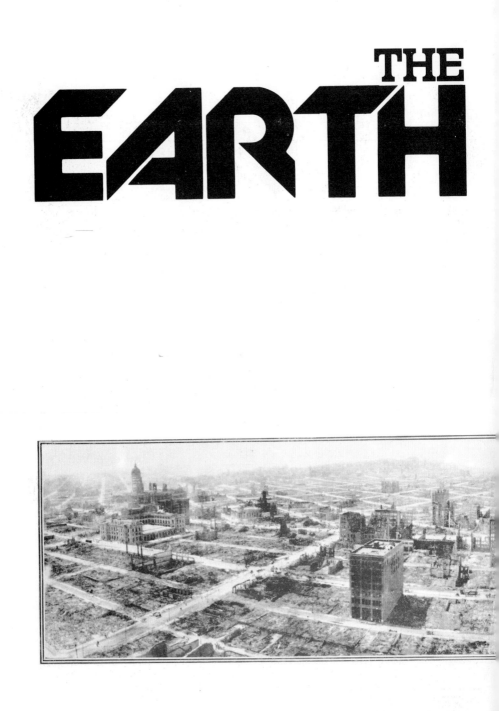

# QUAKE
## HANDBOOK

## Peter Verney

PADDINGTON
PRESS LTD

NEW YORK & LONDON

PREVIOUS PAGES San Francisco after
the earthquake and fire of 1906

Illustrated London News

**Library of Congress Cataloging in Publication Data**

Verney, Peter, 1930–
    The earthquake handbook.

    Bibliography: p.
    Includes index.
    1. Earthquakes.    I. Title.
QE534.2.V47    363.3'4    78-10762

ISBN 0 7092 0836 7
ISBN 0 448 23116 6 (U.S. and Canada only)

Copyright © 1979 Peter Verney
All rights reserved
Filmset in England by SX Composing Ltd., Rayleigh, Essex
Printed and bound in the United States.
Designed by Sandra Shafee

**IN THE UNITED STATES**
PADDINGTON PRESS
Distributed by
GROSSET & DUNLAP

**IN THE UNITED KINGDOM**
PADDINGTON PRESS

**IN CANADA**
Distributed by
RANDOM HOUSE OF CANADA LTD.

**IN SOUTHERN AFRICA**
Distributed by
ERNEST STANTON (PUBLISHERS) (PTY.) LTD.

**IN AUSTRALIA AND NEW ZEALAND**
Distributed by
A. H. & A. W. REED

# Contents

# Introduction

The suddenness of an Earthquake that comes at an instant, unthought of, without warning, that seems to bring unavoidable death along with it, is able to touch an adamantine heart. To see death stalking o'er a great city, ready to sweep us all away, in an instantaneous ruin without a single moment to recollect our thoughts; this is Fear without remedy; this is Fear beyond battle and pestilence. The lightning and thunderbolt, the arrow that flieth by day, may suddenly take off an object or two, and leave no space for repentance; but what horror can equal that when above a million of people are liable to be buried, in one common grave.

The Reverend William Stukeley

IT HAS BEEN ESTIMATED that over seven million people have lost their lives in earthquakes. In 1976 it is believed that the catastrophic earthquake in China alone accounted for over 650,000 deaths. Seismologically speaking, 1977 was a still year, yet well over 3,000 people were killed and countless thousands made homeless in countries as far apart as Iran, Rumania, and the Philippines. The suffering of earthquake victims and survivors alike was indescribable.

There are now indications that the planet Earth is moving into an era of increasing earthquake activity. America waits for the "Big One" that experts agree is bound to strike California sooner or later, for beneath the peaceful countryside, and the many bustling cities of the West Coast, lurk the notorious San Andreas and Hayward faults, amongst others.

In another part of the world, in 1923, an earthquake struck Tokyo and Yokohama, causing over 150,000 deaths and laying waste the better part of both cities; first, in a series of shattering earth tremors; subsequently in a raging firestorm which finished nature's job. It is estimated that a similar quake repeated today would, at a single blow, transform Japan from a thriving nation to one struggling for industrial survival.

It is not a question of *if*, but *when* a major earthquake will strike again. We are nearer to effective prediction, but it remains far from infallible. Control of earthquakes, and even their prevention, is not beyond the reach of human capability, but we are still only at the beginning stages. Today we must rely on using the knowledge we possess to help minimize the effects of disaster.

This is not a technical book: those wanting detailed scientific information should consult some of the many excellent works available, a selection of which are listed in the bibliography. My interest has been to explain the mysteries of this extraordinary natural phenomenon, referring to the records of past earthquakes, and in the light of modern progress in seismology, to help those who may live in or visit one of the many earthquake-prone areas of the world.

A great many people have helped in the writing of this book, but my chief thanks are due to Professor Nicholas Ambraseys, Professor of Engineering Seismology, at the Imperial College of Science and Technology, London, and to Carl A. von Hake of the National Oceanic and Atmospheric Administration, Boulder, Colorado, for their assistance in many areas. I would also like to thank John Germond of Commercial Union, Ron Bishop of the Phoenix Assurance Company, and the Embassy of the People's Republic of China.

# 1
# The Unquiet Earth

THE EASTER CELEBRATIONS were just over. While San Francisco, Pride of the West, a bustling city of half a million, was settling down again to the wearying business of trade and prosperity, music lovers were enjoying a treat of a rare order – a visit by the celebrated Metropolitan Opera Company with the great Caruso and one of the finest basses in the world, Rossi, singing on the same program.

April 18, 1906 broke with a serene dawn, and soon the early morning mist dispersed before a gentle breeze to give promise of another clear day in the brilliant Californian sun. Then precisely at thirteen minutes past five o'clock in the morning the city appeared to shudder. The shaking lasted for sixty-five seconds. There was a pause, for ten seconds, and then an earthquake of shattering intensity struck. (Some reckoned that it lasted for two and a half minutes; others that the duration was three and a half minutes.)

For the first seconds, San Franciscans, long used to lesser earthquakes, thought that this was just another minor tremor. Then as a deep rumbling rose from the earth beneath their feet, it was clear that this time nature meant her worst.

At that time of the morning the streets were largely deserted. There was only the occasional reveler, the milkman going his rounds, the policeman on his beat and a few early workers making their way to their daily toil. One man literally saw the earthquake coming down the street toward him, in great billows like the waves of the sea. Others were thrown to the ground and pinned there as though by some malignant unseen force. As the street weaved and twisted, a horse pulling a dray was knocked off its feet, the driver flung violently against the dashboard. Another cart was crushed to match-wood by a falling telegraph pole.

A city newspaperman, James Hopper, was asleep in his house at the time. He woke suddenly. "My head on the pillow watched my stretched and stiffened body dance. It was springing up and down and from side to side. The bureau at the back of the room came toward me. It danced, approaching not directly, but in a zigzag course, with sudden bold advances and as shy retreats – with little bows and becks and nods, with little mincing steps; it

California Street after the earthquake
and fire of 1906.

was almost funny." Another said that he saw, he was quite positive, the floor circling one way then the other. Then he felt himself picked up and shaken as a terrier does a rat. Someone else said that it was as though a giant had picked up his house and struggled a bit with the weight before dumping it into eternity.

Katharine Hulme, the novelist, wrote in her autobiography, "A far grumble of earth roared beneath the house under our feet. A crack opened in the wall and under our gaze spread like a vein down to the slat beneath the plaster. We fled down the hall past lurching pictures and stopped in terror as some Alaskan harpoons fell from the antler prongs. . . ."

Across San Francisco the rumble of the earth, the deafening roars of falling masonry and tumbling walls drowned all other noise. The houses "reeled and tumbled like playthings." Then it was succeeded by a tense, expectant silence broken only by the bells in those churches still standing as they tolled, driven by the unseen hand of the earthquake. In moments Market Street was piled high with debris, and the roadways buckled and heaved leaving street car tracks suspended high in the air.

The Palace Hotel was a scene of turmoil as terrified residents rushed down from the upper floors in an amazing array of nightwear. And the streets were filling with people.

In their rush, most had grasped at the nearest thing to hand, irrespective of use or value. One held a Bohemian glass bowl, several were clutching bird cages still containing parrots or canaries. One man was seen wearing three hats. One was cradling an alarm clock, yet another clung to a coal scuttle as though it was his most precious possession on earth. Wandering in the streets was a man driven out of his mind by the great disaster. Lost and confused, he raised his hands to heaven and shouted, "The Lord sent it. The Lord sent it." And already across the city in a dozen different places flickers of flame could be seen, as gas mains fractured and wooden beams and rafters fell across open fires – the seeds of the inferno which was to ravage the city.

At six A.M. Pacific Time, a terse, vivid message had come over the Post Office line telling America of the disaster which had struck the greatest city of the west coast. "There was an earthquake at five-fifteen this morning," the operator reported, "wrecking several buildings, and wrecking our offices. They are carting dead from the fallen buildings. There is no water, and we have lost our power. I'm going to get out of the office as we have had a little shake every few minutes, and it's me for the simple life." But the line stayed open for six more hours until, at twenty past two that afternoon, with the flames almost upon the building the line went dead. All communication with the outside world was cut off.

As the rumbling ceased and the earth became still once more, tourist parties began to wander about the city, astonished at the incredible devastation all about them. The four-story Valencia Hotel had collapsed as though flattened by a giant hand. Only the upper floor remained intact, the other three had given way crushing the life from those inside – fifty people perished in this one building alone. The damage was greatest in the low-lying business section of the city. Here land had been reclaimed from the bogs and marshes around the bay, ravines and creeks had been filled in with rocks and rubble, sand and earth. On the "made" land destruction was almost total. The wooden shanty world of Chinatown had almost all collapsed at the first tremor. It was later found that much of this area had actually sunk by as much as three inches (7.6 cm). Where building had taken place on solid rock, damage was inclined to be slight, but throughout the state the greatest area of damage was along the San Andreas fault, in a band up to fifty miles (80 km) wide.

There were many secondary effects. Earth avalanches – dry landslides – occurred in many places, particularly in Humboldt County. A number of earthflows took place, the most notable when an entire hillside slid down a shallow valley for a distance of half a mile (0.8 km) in the space of three remarkable minutes. An earth-slump of monumental proportions happened south of Cape Fortunas when a hill slid bodily into the sea to create a new cape. Lamps suspended from ceilings swung to and fro at a distance of 370 miles (595 km) from San Francisco, while fissures and water jets appeared in many districts. The sea effects were comparatively minor. Although the San

Andreas fault at its northern end runs into the ocean, earth movement here was slight and tide effects could be measured in a few inches rather than feet. To ships at sea, the shock was distinct and intense up to 150 miles (242 km) from the coast; while in irrigation canals, pools and ponds at distances up to 240 miles (386 km) from the epicenter the water was reported to have been violently agitated.

Building damage was intense in many places. The town of Santa Rosa, fifty miles (80 km) north of San Francisco, was almost entirely wrecked. But it was in San Francisco itself that the most extreme damage was caused, for almost all the buildings in the downtown part of the city were destroyed or structurally weakened, and the few that survived the quake were destroyed utterly by the subsequent fire. There were strange sights in San Francisco after the quake. The great City Hall, pride of the City and which had cost $7 million to construct, was left gaunt and bare as the stonework had been shaken from the great elevated dome to leave only a framework of steel. On Mission Street a dozen cattle had been killed by falling debris – they were later roasted by the advancing fire. All over San Francisco people were to be seen dragging to safety trunks containing all they valued and could cram into them. One man reckoned that his most vivid recollection of the entire disaster was the squeak, squeak, squeak of metal trunks being pulled along asphalt.

Then, a new menace struck. With fuel and gas connections broken, electric wires down and sparking wildly, chimneys – some of which had not been swept in years and were full of soot – falling into the fires beneath, stoves over-

City Hall, pride of San Francisco, was left little more than a naked framework of steel.

Illustrated London News

turning and with chemicals spilt, mixed and ignited, in a matter of minutes upward of thirty fires in widely scattered parts of the city were beginning to lick, gather strength and burn.

The Fire Department's widely respected chief, Dan Sullivan, wakened by the first tremor, had rushed to his wife's room only to fall to his death three stories down through a hole in the floor. Although missing his leadership, firemen rushed out the fire engines and hurried through the debris-laden streets. They hitched their hoses to the nearest water hydrant and waited for the expected flow. They waited in vain, only a thin trickle came forth and that soon died completely. Although no one knew it at the time, all three water conduits into the city had been fractured within seconds of the final tremor.

Calling on any supply of water they could find – pools, reservoirs, tanks on the roofs of buildings, even a salt water main although its pumping station had been put out of action by the quake – the firemen found that these sparse supplies were soon exhausted. With no water the highly trained men at the Fire Department were helpless; dumbly they watched San Francisco burn. The city was doomed. The fires which started on the water-front and in Market Street remained isolated for several hours. Had water been available much of San Francisco might have survived, battered but unburned. But then, according to the records, what went down in the city's annals as the "Ham and Eggs Fire" began on the far side of Van Ness Avenue – a part of the city where the houses were predominantly of wood.

With the worst of the earthquake apparently over, a housewife decided

The ground subsided under this
timber house.                      Illustrated London News

By ten o'clock on the morning of April 18, 1906 – five hours after the first tremor – the flames had gathered strength and the greater part of San Francisco was doomed. A panorama taken from Mason Street.

around ten o'clock that some breakfast was overdue. She lit a fire, not realizing that the chimney above had collapsed. In moments the chimney, then the roof, then the whole building was ablaze, and fanned by a gentle breeze the conflagration soon spread to other wooden buildings in the block, until the whole sector of the city was one blazing mass. The fire was spreading.

With the wholesale destruction of San Francisco now imminent, the only solution was to try to clear a fire path to check the racing flames. Prompt use of dynamite was the answer and when the dynamite ran out, the Fire Department, and troops rushed in to help, resorted to gunpowder – which occasionally, in unskilled hands, only resulted in the fire spreading. By the second morning San Francisco was an inferno; and the fire raged for three days and two nights.

A reporter on the *San Francisco Bulletin* wrote, "The most dreadful feature of the whole panorama was the intense silence and the intense motion – the colors were neither those of day or night, but fierce vivid, frenzied tones unimaginable outside the crater of a volcano. The background was a sulky and lurid glow like the unearthly flush on the face of a dying man." Indeed, a casual observer might have thought San Francisco was dying.

Surrounded by fire on three sides, and despite the heroic efforts of the staff to save the building, the great Palace Hotel, symbol of western magnificence and, as many declared, the finest hotel in the world, eventually had to be abandoned when its roof tanks ran dry.

From the refugee camps in the hills, the whole conflagration could be seen in all its awesome magnificence, as four square miles (10.4 sq km) of San Francisco burned unchecked. One wrote afterward: "A sea of liquid fire lay beneath us. The sky above it seemed to burn at white heat, deepening into gold and orange and spreading into a fierce glare. The smoke had gathered

into one gigantic cloud that hung motionless, sharply outlined against a vast field of exquisite starry blue. The streets were caverns of darkness but here and there from the impenetrable gloom three or four houses seemed to stand out like an illuminated card, every cornice and window shining with the reflected blaze.

"As the night advanced it grew cold, and men and women walked up and down between the lines of sleepers, stretching their stiff limbs. Eyes blood-shot with weariness and the pain from the constant rain of cinders, tried to turn away from the fire, but it held them in a dreadful fascination. Now it slipped in and out flowing like a river, engulfing here a church, there a block of houses. A steeple flaring high like a torch toppled and fell in a shower of sparks."

Not until an earthquake has been experienced, and the awesome power of the forces of nature has been revealed in all its naked ferocity, can the ordinary person have any idea what an earthquake really means. Those living in "earthquake country" are used to frequently adjusting pictures on the wall, and the sight of water in the sink slopping about due to some un-seen force. But when a major earthquake comes, they realize that it is like no other experience on this earth.

To modern minds, an earthquake is awesome enough, but to primitive peoples with no understanding of natural forces at work, it was terrifying in its simplicity, in its inevitability, and in its ferocious power.

The ancients were amazed by the natural phenomena of their world. There were mystifying ones like the weather, hot springs, rock formations and eclipses; or terrifying ones like the volcanic eruptions and the earth-quakes which, from time to time, and with devastating effect, ravaged their lands and threw down their cities. It was quite beyond rational compre-

It is hard to imagine that this solid, cloud-shrouded globe is shaken more than one million times a year by earth tremors – one every half minute.

(A remarkable photograph from Apollo 17 during NASA's final lunar mission in 1972).

NASA

hension. They saw waves breaking on the shore as the foaming horses of Poseidon, and the white crests on the sea as the fleeces of the sheep of Proteus who minded the flocks of the sea god.

The early Greeks pictured the earth as being flat and centered at Delphi, its *omphalos* or navel. Others thought of it as drum-shaped. It was difficult to visualize that earth hung in space. Hesiod, a poet who was also a dabbler in the ways of nature, saw the earth as a flat disc floating on water. A popular theory was that the earth covered the air beneath like a lid which, from time to time was subject to ructions from below. The Greek philosophers, Pythagoras and Aristotle, imagined that the world was spherical, while Eratosthenes, who lived in the second century B.C., actually measured the circumference of the earth to within an error of less than 656 feet (200 m) – an incredible achievement. But these were small voices heard by few, and understood only by the most learned.

Strabo, a Greek geographer, who was sixty-three at the birth of Christ, believed that Sagres, at Cape St. Vincent, the southern most point of Portugal, was the end of the earth – "the most westerly point of the inhabited

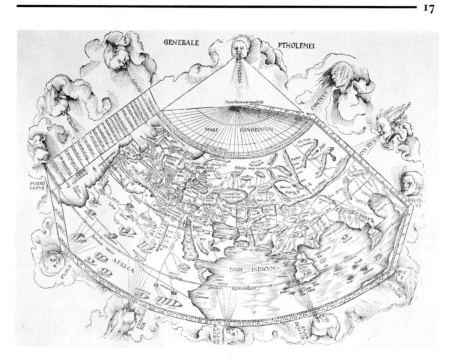

In ancient times, the world was believed to consist of only three continents: Europe, Asia and Africa. (An early sixteenth-century map based on the map drawn up by the geographer Ptolemy). British Library

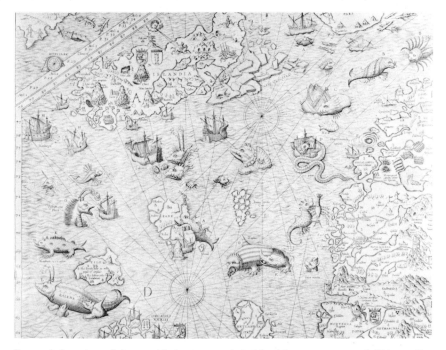

Beyond the edge of the world there was believed to be a frightening void inhabited by monsters and "beastes" of all sorts. British Library

world" it was called. Beyond lay a frightening void, peopled by "beastes" and monsters of all sorts. After that came a rim, *ultima thule*, where the water cascaded away into the unknown.

It was ridiculous, many asserted, to assume that the world was round, and to Lactantius Firmanius, tutor to the son of Constantine the Great, first Christian Emperor of Rome, the whole thing was preposterous. "Is there anyone so foolish," he thundered, "as to believe that there are antipodes with their feet opposite ours; people who walk with their heels upward and their heads hanging down? That there is a part of the world where the trees grow with their branches downwards; and where it rains and snows upwards?" Such a thought was not only inconceivable, it was against the doctrines of the Church, for how could nations in the antipodes be descended from Adam when it was impossible for them to have crossed the intervening ocean?

By the Middle Ages, learned men knew that the earth was a sphere. Further, seamen and those who lived on the coast had daily evidence of the curvature of the earth, for they could watch ships receding over the horizon, until only the tops of the masts could be seen. However, those who lived inland were harder to convince. Most, had they been asked, would have unhesitatingly averred that the earth was flat, and nothing could have persuaded them otherwise. So the shape of the world remained a mystery to some for centuries. Equally puzzling was the nature of the earth itself.

To our ancestors, there was nothing so frightening and inexplicable as

To our ancestors, earthquakes were wholly incomprehensible and terrifying.  (A woodcut of an earthquake in 1613).
Radio Times Hulton Picture Library

when the solid and reassuring earth suddenly started to shake. Buildings collapsed before their eyes, roofs caved in and walls disintegrated in piles of dust. There were mysterious water spouts and other strange phenomena, and the ground heaved, threatening to engulf them.

These upheavals of nature appeared remote to the ordinary man in England in the early part of the eighteenth century, and they mainly afflicted, he was gratified to notice, the "Heathen" parts of the world whose inhabitants doubtless richly deserved this expression of God's displeasure. "We cannot wonder," smugly wrote a divine, "if the concernedness of the Heathen world upon such violent motions of the earth did degenerate into super-stition. Owning a multiplicity of gods, they knew not to which of 'em to ascribe such events."

It was wholly proper, in the words of a popular jingle that "Jamaica shou'd be shook! And lands like Sodom, all impure," or, "That Earthquakes rock Italic ground, Scarce strikes us with Amaze!"

This composure and complacency was to be rudely shattered. The first event which brought about this change was the London earthquake of 1750; the second was the great Lisbon disaster five years later. It was this latter catastrophe, in particular, which was to provide the spur needed to excite the study of earthquakes. (The new science later came to be called seis-mology, from the Greek *seismos* meaning "trembling earth.")

From time to time, earthquakes had been known to strike in England and Scotland, Wales, and more rarely in Ireland, but these were infrequent events, of interest, but of no special consequence. They were certainly no cause for fear or panic, or had not been until around midday on February 8, 1750, when a minor tremor struck London. Lawyers left the courts as the buildings appeared ready to fall about their ears. In Grosvenor Square, the terrified occupants of the houses ran into the streets as their chairs rocked on the floor and pewter rattled on the shelves. There were no casualties, but a lamplighter nearly fell off his ladder.

The earthquake was a mild one, which roused enquiry and speculation rather than alarm. The evangelist John Wesley commented in his journal, "How gently does God deal with this Nation! O, that our repentance may prevent heavier marks of His displeasure."

"Heavier marks" were on the way. One month to the day, on March 8, a second tremor struck the city. This was a more severe event. Two prelimin-ary shocks occurred between one and two o'clock in the morning – "shiver-ing fits," one correspondent called them. Then, at half-past five all London awoke with a start as the city began to shake. One old lady believed that the shaking was caused by her servant falling out of bed; others reckoned it must be an explosion of a powder magazine similar to the one which had taken place nine years before. Within a short space of time, the capital was seething with rumor and counter-rumor, but casualties and damage were slight. A few of the older houses were thrown down, and chimneys by the dozen were either demolished altogether or so weakened that they had to be repaired. China and glass seemed to have been the chief sufferers except for a maid whose arm was broken when she was flung out of bed. Horace Walpole, the diarist and author, wrote to a friend ". . . on a sudden I felt my bolster lift up my head; I thought somebody was getting from under my bed, but soon found it was a strong earthquake, that lasted near half-a-minute with violent vibration and great roaring . . ." All over London church bells rang of their own accord while at Lambeth a pot house lost its roof.

Although a mild shock indeed, the second tremor brought Londoners sharply to their religious senses, for everyone saw that the event could be nothing less than a judgment. Preachers on the following Sunday rose joyfully to the occasion. Their congregations emerged from the lambasting in church and chapel considerably more shaken than by the earthquake itself. "What is God going to do next?" declared one of his disciples, "Will he order winds to tear up our houses from their foundations and bury us in the ruins? Will he remove the raging distemper from cattle and send the plague upon ourselves? Or (the Lord in His infinite mercy save us!) he may command the earth to open her mouth, and, the next time he ariseth to shake terribly the earth, command her to swallow us up alive, with our houses, our wives, our children, with all that appertains unto us." "Indeed . . ." another said, "we are now deservedly alarmed and, for aught we know, may receive a peremptory summons that *we cannot play with* . . . to walk into eternity in the twinkling of an eye, whether sleeping or waking, who can tell?"

William Whiston, a divine and scientist, saw that the end of the world was nigh and that this imminent event would be declared by ninety-nine tokens or signals. He cheerfully pointed out that "vastly the greater part" of these had already taken place. Number ninety-two was to be a terrible, but to "good men, a very joyful great earthquake, when a tenth part of an eminent city will be destroyed," and seven thousand men of name and note would perish. Whiston was not taken very seriously. A contemporary declared that the only mischief the earthquake seemed to have done was to widen the crack in "old Will's noddle." Whiston's preaching stuck closely however to the general train of other sermons, and hanging in the air was the awful realization that the second, the last shock, had taken place precisely one calendar month after the first.

London's fears became crystallized in a pamphlet published eight days after the quake by Doctor Thomas Sherlock, Bishop of London. Walpole turned upon it in wrath, "You never read so impudent, so absurd a piece!" he thundered. "This earthquake which has done no hurt in a country where no earthquake ever did any is sent according to the Bishop to punish bawdy prints, bawdy books . . . gaming, drinking, and all other Sins natural or not . . ." Although Walpole was not impressed, others most certainly were. Under the bombardment of ecclesiastical broadsides, people began to leave London. Townhouses were closed. A hankering for country air and to

The earthquake that never was. Panic-stricken Londoners fleeing from the earthquake predicted for April 5, 1750. That day, according to one cynical observer, seven hundred coaches were seen leaving the city – spurred by the exhortations of a lunatic Lifeguardsman (seen here on the right brandishing a sword marked Prophecy). British Museum

see the spring away from London became a common malady. "They say they are not frightened," Walpole wrote, "but that it is such fine weather." At first the exodus was surreptitious. People pretended that their presence was urgently required elsewhere, or that pressing matters of business took them out of town, but when a certain eccentric Lifeguardsman called Mitchell started to speak in public of the strange coincidence in the dates of the two previous shocks, and pointed out that the month's anniversary of the quakes was all but upon them, the movement became a panic rush. Walpole watched it all with wry amusement. "Within these three days seven hundred and thirty coaches have been counted past Hyde Park Corner with whole parties removing to the country," he wrote.

Those that remained sewed "earthquake gowns" ready for the time when they would be sleeping in the open, while the example of three noble ladies was cited. This gallant trio everyone heard would "go this evening to an inn ten miles out of town where they are to play at brag [a popular card game] till five o'clock in the morning and then come back," as Walpole mused, to look for the bones of their husbands and families under the rubbish.

By April 3 – two days from the date all dreaded – excitement and near-hysteria had hit London. So contagious was the panic that many formerly stout-hearted citizens who had determined to ride out the rumors, also came to the conclusion that it would be foolish to do nothing in face of such a transparent warning of forthcoming doom. It was estimated that one hundred thousand Londoners slept out during the earthquake scare in fields, open spaces or in boats on the river, while one-third of the entire population of the city had fled. Although this figure was a wide exaggeration, an exodus such as London had not seen in many a long day certainly did take place. In Hyde Park, a vast apprehensive throng spent a miserable night in the open in bitter weather, thundered at by the men of God who had never enjoyed so receptive, or so captive, an audience. Others were defiant in face of danger. Certain ladies were so flippant and were "so deliberately, so ludicrously profane in these awful judgments" as to send out invitations to "earthquake parties." At White's Club, a well-known gentleman's club, a scandalized visitor observed that the inmates were actually wagering on the earthquake. "I protest," he declared "that they are such an impious set of people, that if the last trumpet was to sound, they would bet puppet show against Judgment." Another gentleman simulated the watchman's voice and went round banging on doors announcing in sepulchral tones, "Past four o'clock and a dreadful earthquake."

April 5 passed peacefully, as did the following days – for it was not at all clear if the Almighty was using a twenty-eight-day time factor, or a month of thirty or even thirty-one days. The Lifeguardsman was thrown into Bedlam as being completely unhinged and those who had left town started to creep back sheepishly to be greeted by a barrage of teasing from those who remained.

The *Gentleman's Magazine* had a field day. An anonymous poet wrote in its pages:

> Come – come out of your holes, for you've got a reprieve,
>> O ye Sons and ye Daughters of Adam and Eve;
> Like that naughty *pair*, by your voices confounded,
>> Without quiet – without shame – with sorrow surrounded,
> You have fled from the call, unreform'd tho' afraid,
>> When *the voice of the Lord* was in earthquakes convey'd
> O wonderful work of a reasoning creature!

The magazine followed this up with an editorial: "So far, even to their wits' end, had their superstitious fears, or their guilty conscience driven them." The *Daily Advertiser* was round in its condemnation: "How stupid panics speak a pigmy race." Sober sense was expounded by another journal, "Let such weak minds consider that when God resolves to punish a sinful nation, He alone knows the proper time of doing it . . . a time that no human sagacity could ever foresee or foretell."

The Devil – writing anonymously – contributed a letter congratulating the people of Britain in general and of London in particular. He wrote, "Before, we had known not which is most worthy of our admiration, whether your unparalleled refinements in all kinds of luxury and debauchery, or your sagacity in reasoning away every principle of virtue and honour . . . France and Rome compared to you are but petty candidates for Hell."

If the London earthquake had concentrated people's minds wonderfully, although only briefly, on the mysteries of nature, it was the Lisbon earthquake five years later which truly brought home to an astonished civilized world how puny were their efforts in face of those of the Almighty.

In 1755, Lisbon, capital of Portugal, was a thriving city. Lying on the northern side of the River Tagus, about six miles (9.6 km) from its mouth, Lisbon was built on the slopes of a low range of hills. It possessed a population nearing a quarter of a million and the city itself sprawled across an area some four miles (6.5 km) long and one and a half miles (2.4 km) wide. Most of the houses were of stone, some as much as four or even five stories in height, while many of the streets were narrow and steep.

Lisbon was enjoying a fabulous prosperity. It was this fact, tinged with more than a little envy, which so shattered people when they heard of the great earthquake which ravaged the city on All Saints Day, 1755, for Lisbon was one of the busiest ports in all Europe, the wealth of its merchants legendary. Portugal was still glorying in the fame of its explorers and discoveries, basking in the luxury brought about by the immense wealth of its South American colonies, wealth which was channeled through Lisbon. The capital was renowned as a seat of learning. In its magnificent libraries lay priceless documents and papers dealing with the history of Portugal's great past.

Source of merchant wealth, seat of learning and study, Lisbon had a less

"I beheld the city waving backwards and forwards like a cornfield in a breeze." The Lisbon earthquake of

All Saints Day, 1755 as seen from the River Tagus.

Radio Times Hulton Picture Library

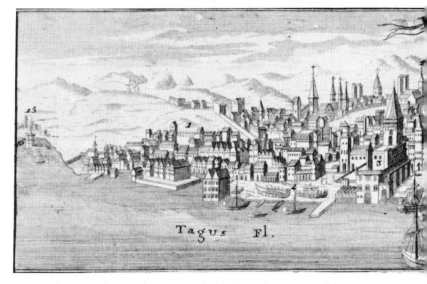

Lisbon the fair. A contemporary panorama of the great Portuguese capital before the catastrophic earthquake of 1755.

envied reputation as the home of the dreaded Inquisition. Religion ruled the lives of the people. There were more than forty parish churches and over ninety convents. It was a city of many medieval houses next to more substantial palaces and buildings, many of soft pinkish marble.

Lisbon and the surrounding area were no strangers to earthquakes before the great one struck that November day. Between the year A.D. 1000 and the mid-eighteenth century, there had been upward of a dozen quakes, some more severe than others, but all sufficiently noteworthy to cause damage. One, in 1531, was thought to have destroyed over a thousand houses and all the churches, and was succeeded by a mighty tidal wave which completed the destruction. Twenty years later another wrecked two hundred houses and caused the death of ten times as many Lisboans. But none of the previous earthquakes remotely compared with the great shock of 1755.

Dutifully, on the morning of All Saints Day, the good people of Lisbon made their way to church. The day was clear, and very still, the sun was bright but the more observant later remembered that there was a thin haze, like breath upon glass. Suddenly, without warning, at forty minutes past nine, there was a "strange, frightful noise underground, resembling the hollow distant rumbling of thunder," wrote one survivor, and he watched helpless while his house was tossed from side to side "with a motion like that of a waggon driven violently over rough stones."

In another part of the city a young English merchant was talking to two Portuguese friends in the counting house. "Suddenly," he wrote, "we found the house shake, and a great Noise like a Coach and Six driving by; we stared at each other; They said it was a Coach; I answered none came through our street; that we were all lost; It was certainly a violent Earthquake, and I

---

desired them to follow me. An instant thought took me, that it was a general Perdition, or may be the last Day; but if there was Safety, it would be under the Stone Arch. . . ." Another young man, one Thomas Chase, described it as "the most dreadful jumbling noise that ears ever heard."

In the churches the priests had begun the introit, *Gaudeamus omnes in Deo* when the walls "began to suddenly rock and sway like an unsteady ship at sea," the heavy chandeliers to swing with increasing violence above the heads of the terrified congregations.

Panic-stricken, they fled into the streets, many clutching images before them and fell to their knees in supplication. As they knelt and as Lisbon swayed around them, another, more violent shock struck the city. This lasted a full three minutes. The buildings, cracked and weakened by the first shock could stand no more, and many fell into the streets below and crushed those who had run out of the churches. "Numbers expired then," wrote an Englishman, "and others with the Clergy running about over the Ruins to confess and absolve them who were still alive – all shouting to God for Mercy."

The result of the second shock was witnessed by another merchant. "There was a high-arched passage," he wrote afterward, "like one of our city gates, fronting on the west door of the ancient cathedral; on the left was the famous church of St. Anthony and on the right some private houses, several storeys high. . . . At the first shock, numbers of people, who were then passing under the arch, fled into the centre of the area; those in the two churches, as many as could possibly get out, did the same. At this instant the arched gateway, with the fronts of the two churches and the contiguous buildings, all inclined one towards the other with the violence of the shock, fell down and buried every soul as they were standing there crowded together."

In an instant, the city was shrouded in the thickest dust, darker than night, and the screams of the injured added another unholy dimension to the scene. At the second shock those on the edge of the city ran to the fields, those in the center to any open space, particularly along the banks of the Tagus. Then, to complete the terror came horrified shouts of "the sea is coming."

Among the assembled shipping at the mouth of the Tagus was a British merchant ship. At the first shock, as the captain described, "I felt the ship have an uncommon Motion, and could not help thinking she was aground, although sure of the Depth of Water. As the Motion increased, my Amazement increased also, and as I was looking round to find out the Meaning of the uncommon Motion, I was immediately acquainted with the direful Cause; when at that Instant looking towards the City, I beheld the tall and stately Buildings tumbling down, with great cracks and Noise." Another ship's captain described the city as "waving backwards and forwards like a cornfield in a breeze."

Along the shore of the Tagus many terror stricken Lisboans had congregated on the newly-built marble quay, the Cais de Pedra. At the second shock, or shortly before it – opinions differ – the whole quay disappeared into the river bearing with it many hundreds of people who had there sought sanctuary, and drawing into the vortex a number of small boats moored alongside. The waves came and went three times, submerging much of the lower part of Lisbon, and completing the destruction wrought by the two earthquakes. Many who were rowing to the south shore seeking safety away from the stricken city were engulfed, and so were the ships anchored in the river or tied to the wharves and quays.

It is probable, however catastrophic the damage caused by the quakes and the seismic waves, that Lisbon could have at least partly survived in its existing form, but soon the battered survivors had another terror facing them – fire.

At the first tremors the many candles on the altars toppled over setting fire to vestments and other church decorations. There was no one to put them out, soon sparkles of flame were licking at the remains of the city in a score of places. And as if the altar candles were not enough, roofs and timbers collapsed into kitchen and hearth fires lit for meals or to provide warmth on a chill November day. Fanned by a steady northeast wind, the fires burned and spread until a huge pall of smoke from a raging inferno hung over the city; beneath it the fire went to work.

Sweeping through houses, churches and palaces with awesome impartiality the fire destroyed an incalculable quantity of furniture, pictures, tapestries, books and manuscripts. The Royal Palace and the fine new Opera House, completed only eight months before, were completely gutted. The priceless records of the India Company were destroyed by the fire. The losses to goods, most of which were burned, were even at eighteenth century prices, computed at the staggering total of near $24 million. In the magnificent Palace of the Marquês de Louriçal, two hundred pictures were burned including fine Titians, Correggios and works by Rubens. In the King's Palace alone it was estimated that seventy thousand books were lost, and other archives with treasures beyond price were all destroyed.

If the material suffering of Lisbon was colossal, the human suffering was vastly worse. "In some places," described one survivor, "lay coaches, with their masters, horses and riders almost crushed to pieces: here mothers with infants in their arms: there ladies richly dressed, friars, gentlemen, mechanics: some had their backs or thighs broken: others vast stones on their breasts: some lay almost buried in the rubbish. Of animals some were killed, some were wounded, but the greater part, which had received no hurt, were left there to starve." Amid the tragedy and chaos someone noticed a young army officer standing lonely vigil outside the mint to prevent the bullion and treasures being stolen by looters.

There were many narrow escapes. One man, Sir Harry Frankland, was riding about the city in his chaise when he suddenly saw his driver look behind him and then lash the mules into a gallop. Very soon both driver and mules were buried in the ruins of a house which fell on them. Sir Harry escaped by plunging through an open doorway. The house in which he sought sanctuary also collapsed, but he escaped serious injury, although it was some time before he was dug out of the rubble. A small child, aged three, was buried to the neck when the house he was in toppled down around him. He emerged saying, "I fell down in the dirt." Less fortunate was the Spanish ambassador, who was crushed under the door of his house as he tried to escape into the street.

Another man described the scene after the fire as "not to be expressed by Human Tongue, how dreadful and how awful it was to enter the City after the fire was abated; when looking upwards one was struck with terror at beholding frightful pyramids of ruined Fronts, some inclining one Way, some another; then on the other hand with Horror in viewing Heaps of Bodies crushed to Death, half-buried and half-burnt; and if one went through the broad places of Squares, there was nothing to be met with but People bewailing their Misfortunes, wringing their Hands and crying. The World is at an end." To add to their misfortunes, a third shock, around noon further terrified the people and toppled some of the few remaining buildings.

By now a rush had started for the hills and fields outside the city. Those that remained, some unable to move due to their injuries, were more frightened of dying unconfessed and unforgiven than of the earthquake itself. Priests, with the utmost composure, moved among the injured and trapped administering the last sacraments and taking a form of mass confession. A Protestant Englishman caught in the press was among those who received the Sacrament, a lesser evil than revealing he was a heretic, for in their current mood the Lisboans were ready to find any cause or culprit for the disaster which had laid waste their beautiful city.

Many believed themselves in the bowels of the earth. "The grinding of the walls, the fall of churches, the lamentable cries of the inhabitants, join'd to a perfect darkness occasion'd by the dust, made one of the dreadfullest scenes of nature," a horrified English merchant wrote, "The terror of the people was beyond description, nobody wept, it was beyond tears; they ran hither and thither, delirious with horror and astonishment, beating their faces and their breasts."

The aftershocks went on and on. They did little damage except bring down a few buildings tottering from the first tremors, but they maintained the general level of hysteria and seemingly justified the many prophets of woe who took the opportunity of predicting that an even worse calamity was imminent and that God had not completed his punishment of the unworthy. Two particularly severe ones took place on December 11 and December 23. "Will your earth never be quiet," wrote the British ambassador at Madrid to the envoy in Lisbon. He wrote with some feeling, for Madrid, three hundred miles (483 km) away from Lisbon had also felt the shocks of the great earthquake.

News of the great Lisbon earthquake was slow to travel, and when people heard of the great disaster that had struck Portugal's capital a number of strange phenomena which had puzzled so many were explained. Never had the repercussions of a natural disaster been so pronounced or widespread. At first the accounts were completely disbelieved – early reports were grossly exaggerated in any case – but gradually it began to dawn that what had taken place had been a natural disaster such as the civilized world had never experienced before. The final death tolls varied between seventy to one hundred thousand, but the true total was never discovered although the most diligent analysis went on after the earthquake – the most thorough to that date.

In fact the effects of the Lisbon earthquake were felt over an area estimated as being over one million and a half square miles (3.86 million sq km). Both sides of the Atlantic recorded remarkable tides. Lakes as far north as Sweden were affected, the River Dal in Norway, 1,800 miles (2,890 km) away overflowed its banks. It was felt in France, Germany, Italy and Switzerland. Chandeliers swung in the town of Fahlun in Sweden, an incredible 1,850 miles (2,980 km) away from Lisbon. In Great Britain, remarkable water effects were recorded, particularly on the southern coast. In Derbyshire, nearly 1,000 miles (1,600 km) away from the epicenter, pieces of plaster fell off walls and a fissure nearly 150 yards (136.5 m) long opened in a field. In Scotland, a preacher giving a sermon was astonished to see his congregation suddenly lurch as though struck by a gust of wind.

The earthquake caused considerable damage in Spain. In Madrid several walls were fractured. At Seville, the tower of the Metropolitan Church, already leaning heavily due to past earthquakes, was incredibly set upright again. At Thionville in the Duchy of Luxembourg, the military barracks were completely demolished and the entire garrison of five hundred men buried in the ruins.

By far the greatest damage was reserved for North Africa. Here the calamity and the casualty list was as great as in Lisbon itself. Morocco and Tangier were hardest hit, while the town of Algiers was almost entirely demolished.

If the physical results of the Lisbon earthquake were dramatic, so were the moral and spiritual ones. The shock was deep-seated; many said that the world would never be the same again. It was a stunning blow beyond the comprehension of most, and as letters and accounts from the survivors started to arrive, the true extent of the calamity became apparent. People were stunned at the immensity of the tragedy. At Cambridge University the Vice Chancellor wrote, "We have been perfectly quiet here, nor have I had certain information of the least irregularity amongst the scholars. It has rather become fashionable to be decent." Another wrote, "Between the French (who were threatening invasion) and the earthquake, you have no notion how good we are grown. Nobody makes a suit now but of sackcloth turned up with ashes."

A public fast day was declared – and kept devoutly. By popular demand, frivolity of all sorts was frowned on. One of the most deeply shaken was the

The casualties in North Africa were almost as bad as those in Lisbon itself. Algiers was all but destroyed and the town of Mequinez – pictured here in an old engraving – ceased to exist.

*Auto da Fé or the Annual Burning of Hereticks at Lisbon*

What had Lisbon done to earn this awful retribution? It wasn't hard to blame the dreaded Inquisition and the inhuman practice of the *Auto da Fé* or annual burning of heretics. A cartoon produced after the Lisbon earthquake of 1755.

British Museum

king of France, who promised to receive the Sacrament at Easter, and give up his mistress. Seeing her favors so lightly cast aside, she pronounced that she would give up rouge as an offering to "the demon of earthquakes."

One of the first acts was to find a saint to protect the realm from further earthquakes. From a small field, St. Francis Borgia, who had died in 1572, was chosen. On the whole he had a good track record in warding off such horrors as earthquakes, but was faced with strong competition from St. Theotonius and the Martyrs of Morocco. St. Agatha was a late entry, who had been enormously successful in dealing with earthquakes and the eruptions of Mount Etna in Sicily. Nevertheless, by special request of the king, Pope Benedict XIV made the appointment of St. Francis in May 1756.

There were tales too of miraculous happenings after the earthquake. A statue of the Virgin Mary was seen amid the engulfing flames, apparently blessing the stricken city and, according to a scurrilous Protestant observer, waving a white handkerchief. People emerged after days under the rubble. A fifteen-year-old girl was found quite unharmed after a lengthy entombment and clutching an image of St. Anthony, patron saint of Lisbon. The corpses of priests struck down in the middle of celebrating mass in their churches were found afterward in a miraculous state of preservation, although bodies nearby were decomposing.

People remembered that the earthquakes had been predicted, and regretted that they had paid no attention. Prophecies and presentiments were recalled. Christ himself, it was said, had told a nun, Maria Joanna, that he was deeply offended by the wickedness of Portugal, particularly by the sins of Lisbon; and he warned that appropriate punishment would be inflicted. Another nun had told her confessor, no less than five times, that something terrible would occur on All Saints Day, 1752. When nothing happened, the portent was transferred to 1753, and again to 1754, by which time people were wearying of the business. Now this miraculous warning was remembered – after all it had only been wrong by four years.

At appropriate anniversaries of the great quake, other catastrophes were predicted. Another was due, so it was said, on the last day of the month, then forty days after November 1, and periodically thereafter. May 1 was a date chosen by one ecclesiastical crank – six months after the tragic event.

The anniversary was universally looked upon with dread, and played on with vigor by the ill-intentioned who were waiting for houses to be abandoned before looting them. By the end of October 1756, the whole city was in a state of jitters. Troops were posted on all routes to prevent anyone leaving, and proclamations warned of the direst retributions to anyone trying to flee the city. To make matters worse, there was a slight shock on the evening of October 29. Public processions were organized to display the national penitence. The king, queen and princesses took part in the first; senior ecclesiastics and town officials led the second, while the Papal Nuncio conducted ceremonial feet-washing ceremonies. For there was little doubt "That the Lord was in the earthquake, and that it was His angel that troubled the waters."

In other countries there was certainly no doubt that those in Lisbon had brought it all upon themselves. The *London Magazine* pointed out that Lisbon might be said to be the most visibly rich and the most abandonedly wicked and superstitious city in the world. A clergyman supported this common view, "Is there a scene," he wrote in an epistle to the people of Lisbon, "of lewdness or debauchery that was ever practised that hath not daily been repeated in your religious houses?" Another uncharitably pointed out that there was no question of the innocent perishing with the guilty, for there were no innocent people in Lisbon.

As if the Portuguese did not have enough troubles of their own, the rest of the world showed little compassion for them. People wondered what terrible crimes that nation had committed that would justify this massive retribution from on high. "Let me beg you to ask yourselves, if there was not some Cause that might justly provoke the God of Heaven tô visit you thus severely?" wrote someone. One reason was popularly scouted: "Think O Spain and Portugal," a correspondent to one of the popular magazines wrote, "the millions of poor Indians your forefathers butchered for the sake of the gold."

The loudest condemnation was reserved for the Inquisition – only the hottest Hell should be their lot. In an orgy of self-righteousness a man of God wrote, "Did not Bigotry and Superstition, Cruelty and Bloodthirstiness appear amongst them, and that in the highest Degree? There stood the INQUISITION, the very mentioning of which is enough to shock an English Ear, where Numbers of Virgins have been sacrificed to the brutal Lusts of those wretched Monsters, the Inquisitors. . . . No wonder that Lisbon is fallen; God has justly made it like unto SODOM and GOMORRAH. . . ." It was pointed out with satisfaction that about the only church left standing in the city was Protestant while the Palace of the Inquisition had been one of the first buildings to be destroyed.

Ecclesiastics fell over themselves in their eagerness to draw soul-shattering conclusions about the moral significance of the great earthquakes. In a pamphlet which was to become a small bestseller and entitled *Serious Thoughts occasioned by the late Earthquake in Lisbon*, John Wesley, the great church reformer, let loose his powerful rhetoric: "It comes! The Roof trembles! The Beams crack! The Ground rocks to and fro! Hoarse Thunder resounds from the Bowels of the Earth! And all these are but the Beginning of Sorrows. Now what Help? What Wisdom can prevent? What Strength resist the Blow? What Money can purchase, I will not say Deliverance, but an Hour's Reprieve?" – and much more in a similar vein.

Such comments caused more embarrassment than contrition. The Archbishop of Canterbury tried to put a stop to the greater ecclesiastical excesses and declared that "a presumptuous forwardness in pronouncing on extraordinary events we leave to raving designing monks, Methodists and ignorant enthusiasts."

Children were not allowed to forget the dire event. A hymn composed especially and recommended to parents for their little ones to learn by heart, "in order to impress on their tender minds an awful sense of their Creator's omnipotence in the late melancholy destruction of Lisbon," included the lines:

> Tho' Earth her ancient Seat forsake,
> By pangs convulsive torn,
> Tho her self-balanced Fabrick shake,
> And ruin'd Nature mourn;
>
> Tho' Hills be in the Ocean lost,
> With all their trembling Load,
> No fear shall e'er disturb the Just,
> Or shake his Trust in God.

Others were quicker to forget. A diarist in London wrote five months after the Lisbon quake, "Earthquakes are forgotten, assemblies and balls go on as briskly as if no such warning had been given; indeed, if we stop there it might be innocent, but luxury of all kinds and gaming run higher than ever."

But the Lisbon earthquake was not forgotten. In 1858 Oliver Wendell Holmes wrote in *A Logical Story, The Deacon's Masterpiece, or the Wonderful "One-Hoss Shay."*

> Seventeen hundred and fifty-five,
> *George Secundus* was then alive,
> Snuffy old drone from the German hive
> That was the year when Lisbon-town
> Saw the earth open and gulp her down . . .
>
> It was on the terrible Earthquake day
> That the Deacon finished the one-hoss shay
> First of November, the Earthquake day
> There are traces of age in the one-hoss shay,
> A general flavor of mild decay . . .
>
> The parson was working his Sunday's text,
> Had got to *fifthly*, and stopped perplexed
> At what the – Moses – was coming next.
> All at once the horse stood still,
> Close by the meetin'-house on the hill.
> First a shiver, and then a thrill
> Then something decidedly like a spill,
> And the parson was sitting upon a rock
> At half past nine by the meetin'-house clock,
> Just the hour of the Earthquake shock . . . .

# 2
# The Great Search
## The Story of Seismology

THE TURMOIL OF SUPERSTITION and quasi-scientific speculation that succeeded the Lisbon earthquake confounded rational consideration of the causes of earthquakes.

At times men had observed steam and other exhalations issuing from below. This must be due, they said, to the working of underground winds, or the release of imprisoned vapors beneath the earth's surface. One man of science in the seventeenth century declared that "the Earth is hollow and broken in many places, and is not one firm and united mass," for this, he reckoned, he had the "Testimony of Sense and of easie Observation to prove," while to another it was reasonable to suppose that in the center of the earth were "many holes and corners, some fill'd with smoak and fire, some with water and some with mouldy Aire."

With terror of the unknown upon them, people turned to the only comfort they knew – religion – and little enough reassurance they found. Their gods were out to wreak retribution, not to succor and comfort the survivors Many a preacher declaimed that man had sinned and must pay the forfeit. Since the earliest days earthquakes were seen as visible acts of a vengeful god. Atlantis, the legendary city, was seen as paying the penalty for manifold misdeeds, and so banished beneath the waves. The original "City of the Damned," the former pirate haunt, Port Royal in Jamaica, was wholly destroyed by an earthquake in 1692, an act, surely of a wrathful god? In 1822, when a succession of earthquakes shook Chile, priests sought to persuade their flocks that this was God's opinion of the revolutionary fervor then raging through South America. As recently as 1930, an Italian bishop declared that an earthquake that summer was due to the immodesty of women's dress and the general immorality of the people.

Apart from a general moral unworthiness, certain specific acts were sometimes thought to bring on earthquakes. It was gleefully pointed out – by those who were not there – that the earthquake which destroyed much of Pompeii and Herculaneum in A.D. 62, before the great eruption of Vesuvius which smothered both towns, had struck when the people were at their diversions in the theater. In the sixth century, the Roman Emperor Justinian decreed that those uttering blasphemy, and thus causing earthquakes and thunderbolts, would suffer the death penalty. Earlier, his predecessor Theodosius, had forecast imminent bloody eclipses, demons of hell, fighting sea monsters and, for good measure, earthquakes if the people did not mend their ways. These words were taken to heart. As confirmation that earthquakes were the direct act of vengeful gods, preachers hastened to point out that earthquakes only struck at the centers of sin – the cities – and not toward "desarts and uninhabited places," conveniently forgetting that in such spots the occurrence of an earthquake was likely to pass unnoticed anyway. In 1752, the most learned scientific body in England, the Royal Society, profoundly declared that "earthquakes only occur when people need chastening." Earlier civilizations held other views.

In Scandinavian mythology the god Loki, having killed his brother Balder, is bound to a rock while a serpent slowly drops poison on to his up-turned face. Loki's wife catches most of the poison in a dish but when the dish is full and she must go away to empty it, the poison falls on her husband's face causing him to writhe and shake the earth.

In the legends of the Maoris of New Zealand, the God Ru is left with his parent, Papa, Mother of Earth, still in her womb or at her breast. He is a restless offspring; when he stirs he causes earthquakes; when he turns over the seasons change. Mayan mythology tells of the earth being cube-shaped and supported at the corners by four gods, the Vashakmen, who, whenever in their opinion the world becomes overpopulated, tip it to get rid of surplus humanity. A rather charming vision of the earth is found in Rumanian legend, which sees the world as resting on the three divine pillars of Faith, Hope and Charity. When one falters, the earth shakes.

In Japan, considered by many as virtually the home of the earthquake, the cause was either an "earthquake insect," a sort of scale-covered spider called *Jushin mushi*, which caused the earth to shake whenever it stirred, or a great catfish which was curled under the sea and on whose back rested the four islands, while its head and tail resided under a large rock in the sea.

Seventeen years before the eruption of Vesuvius engulfed Pompeii and Herculaneum, both towns were severely damaged by an earthquake, commemorated here in a wall frieze.

Professor N.N. Ambraseys

The Algonquins, of North America, believed that the earth was riding, rather insecurely, on the back of a giant tortoise. In Mongolia they reckoned that it rested on a frog. Those who lived in the Celebes of East India saw the world-supporting creature as a hog. In Siberia, the presence of many giant bones led to the belief that under the ground dwelt huge animals, which caused the earth to shudder as they tramped around. In the nearby Kamchatka Peninsula, a god called Tuli drove a sledge pulled by flea-infested dogs; when the dogs stopped to scratch the earth was shaken.

Even now, primitive and not so primitive peoples see earthquakes as having supernatural origins. After a particularly catastrophic earthquake in India near the beginning of the last century a letter asserted to have come from Mecca foretold of the approaching Day of Judgment. The holy men stated that the cause of the earthquakes was the horse Dooldool, which pawed the ground restlessly demanding food with a strangely human appetite – thus all good Muslims were enjoined to send food to keep him contented. For their part the Hindus saw the earthquake as being the result of a quarrel between two mythical sects, the Dyets and Dewas. And when Darwin in his great scientific voyage round the world stopped off in South America, he discovered some people who thought that the recent earthquake which had destroyed their villages was caused by the wrath of some old Indian women who had been offended and stopped up the neighboring volcano.

There was little distinction between earthquakes and volcanoes; both were equally terrifying and inexplicable. The Greek philosophers had little faith in primitive judgments and opinions that they were caused by the wayward behavior of mythical beasts. They believed that earthquakes were due to natural causes, but just what, defeated them. The philosopher Anaxagoras reckoned that the flat earth was kept rotating by a mighty force around it which made it settle in the middle. Within the earth lay a roaring furnace; when this was aroused the earth was thrown about like flotsam on a rough sea, and this caused earthquakes. Thales, who lived half a century later, saw the earth as floating on water. This accounted for the springs and fountains which often spurted forth during earthquakes. Aristotle, who appeared on the scene a century and a half later – and who had the endearing habit of condemning anything with which he disagreed as "simple minded" – believed that somehow the winds of the world – the "pneuma," he called them – were sucked into the interior of the earth and there combined with the noxious gases in the center of the globe either to rush about causing earthquakes, or else to escape as volcanoes. Democritus, Aristotle's elder, blamed rain for causing earthquakes. Lucretius, the Roman poet, however, foretold something akin to modern seismology and pronounced that underground rocks became displaced in subterranean caverns or the hidden recesses of the earth and in falling caused earthquakes.

Not until the early part of the sixteenth century did geological phenomena

For centuries rational "scientific" study was bedeviled by the belief that the world had been created anew at the time of the Flood. (Danby, *The Deluge*)

start once again to be subject to serious investigation. No less than Leonardo da Vinci declared that the mud found in fossil shells had come there when the land was at the bottom of the sea. "They tell us," he wrote, "that these shells were formed in the hills by the influence of the stars: but I ask where in the hills are the stars now forming shells of distinct ages and species? And how can the stars explain the origin of gravel, occurring at different heights and composed of pebbles rounded as if by the motion of running water . . . ?"

Later theorists saw the fossilized shells as sports of nature or "productions formed in imitation of life." A few saw them as the spoils of marine animals. Others believed that they were the product of creatures which had perished in the Flood.

The study of such natural phenomena was wholly confused by the crystallizing of time into one great and catastrophic event – the Flood. The prevailing view was that the life of the earth had been comparatively brief – a few thousand years at most. The Bible clearly showed that the earth was the product of one mighty act of creation; since then Noah's deluge had been the only terrestial event of note. Further, although the date for the expected end of the earth had passed, that end could not now be far off. Indeed, in the Middle Ages, pious men would pass their lands to holy orders under the apprehension that the end of the world was nigh and Judgment Day just around the corner. This adherence to the belief that the world was of brief ancestry and destined to a shorter future was to bedevil

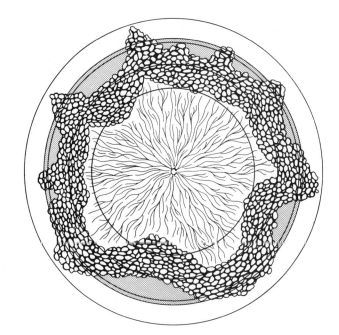

In their frantic search for an explanation of earthquakes, some thought that the earth contained a white-hot, fiery furnace. Cross section of the earth, after a drawing by Abbé Lazzaro Moro, an eighteenth-century man of science.

scientific thinking for centuries, while any suggestion that the Noah episode had not created the world anew and erased all that had gone before was treated as rank heresy. Those who had the temerity to propose that fossilized shells might have once belonged to a marine animal and had predated the deluge by a considerable time, were looked upon with scorn and damned as irreligious, until a general acceptance began to creep in during the eighteenth century that earth might have origins long before the appearance of man.

To men of science in the eighteenth century, the origins of earthquakes remained obscure. Some thought that earthquakes were caused by water which acted "after several Manners; either by dissolving the Salts scattered through the Earth, or by penetrating through porous Lands, mix'd with stones, which they insensibly loosen; and the Fall or Removal thereof must cause a Stroke or Shock, such as is felt in Earthquakes. Lastly, the Water penetrating some sulphurous Bodies must there cause a Fermentation; and then the Heat produces Winds and foul Exhalations, which infect the Air when they open the Earth; whence it is after great Earthquakes abundance of People die." Others saw a chemical reaction going on in the bowels of the earth where the presence of "Pyrites and other pyritous materials" which "occur in greater or less quantity in every place" were easy to blame.

The most popular belief on the cause of earthquakes still revolved around the ancient philosophers' ideas of vapors and strange subterranean winds.

"These hollownesses of the Earth the Ancients made prisons, or storehouses for the winds, and set a God over them to confine them, or let them loose at His pleasure," wrote one "scientist." Others saw the same dreadful hollowness in the belly of the earth and under the roots of mountains, where the "exhalations" struggled to escape their prison – usually through volcanoes which acted as a kind of safety valve. Some thought that beneath the earth ran burrows or channels, clefts or caverns, that "never had the comfort of one beam of light since the great fall of the earth."

Sometimes the "exhalations" issued forth "wholly together; sometimes by laboring it concealeth fire, and breaketh out in flames; other whiles part of it remayneth behinde, and is shutte up again within the earth." These fires in the interior of the earth figured in many interpretations. After all, this was a logical enough deduction from the sight and smell of noxious gases issuing from the land. One theorist came to the conclusion that an accidental obstruction to this subterranean fire caused tremors. Another decided that "all substances which are inflammable and capable of explosion do, like powder at the instant of their inflammation generate a great quantity of air," and this air, compressed by its surroundings, produced most violent effects. The concept of "ethereal fire", "occult fire" or the "subtil fluid" had been propounded by many – the last by Sir Isaac Newton. From this point it was not long before it was pointed out that "fire gives elasticity, and elasticity, or vibration, is the mother of electricity."

As electricity was a convenient solution to many phenomena, so it came to be held as the answer to the cause of earthquakes. It was popularly supposed that the flashes of fire which were widely reported by those experiencing earthquakes must be the ascending earth vapors igniting and creating a sort of earth lightning. Benjamin Franklin pronounced, "if a non-electric cloud discharges its contents on any part of the earth, when in a highly electrified state, an earthquake must necessarily ensue . . . the shock of many miles compass of solid earth must needs be an earthquake: and that snap, from the contact, be the horrible uncouth noise of it."

Another, who experienced the London earthquake, said, "I plainly heard a loud explosion up in the air, like that of a small cannon: which made me conjecture, that the noise was owing to the rushing off, and sudden expansion of the electrical fluid, at the top of St. Martin's spire; where all the electrical effluvia, which ascended up along the larger body of the tower, ebbing by attraction strongly condensed, and accelerated at the point of the weathercock, as they rushed off, made so much the louder expansive explosion."

An English scientist of the period, the Reverend William Stukeley, supported Franklin's theory and he attributed the London earthquake solely to electricity, for the weather beforehand had been warm and dry, broken by a storm, and he too felt that if a non-electric cloud discharged on the earth while the latter was in an "electric" state, an earthquake would inevitably result. He also drew attention to other phenomena to support his thesis;

Others saw certain areas of the earth connected by underground passages and tunnels and visualized earthquakes and volcanic action "stalking round the globe." This tunnel was supposed to run under the northern parts of Norway and Sweden.

British Library

that the Aurora Borealis had been seen much further south than usual; and that near London vegetables had been very forward "and we all know electricity does that."

Although Stukeley was somewhat off-target, he did at least point out that the vapor theory supported by so many of his contemporaries was so much nonsense for, as he said, miners underground never met it, and if there were subterraneous fires, why was it that springs of water did not put them out? But he was careful enough to mention that the reason for earthquakes lay with the Almighty; electricity was only God's agent in the matter.

Indeed there could be no doubt who caused earthquakes; all these "natural" suggestions were purely accidental, said one doubter. There were two objections to that theory, first it was untrue, secondly, it was "uncomfortable" – as it did not conform to religious teaching. In this instance there was no doubt that evil spirits had obtained, God permitting for the time being, malevolent control over the forces of nature.

Still at that period the "chastening hand of God" is behind most interpretations of the earthquake. "Earthquakes generally happen to great towns and cities, and more particularly to those that are situated on the sea, bays and great rivers – the chastening rod is directed to towns and cities, where are inhabitants, the object of its monition; not to bare cliffs and uninhabited beach." Memories of the painful and uncomfortable days of the London earthquake were still fresh in men's minds, and the lack of reports of significant earth movements in country districts signified that this must, surely, be the explanation.

Not many, though, were as composed or as rational as the man who wrote that earthquakes are "part of the ordinary hazards of life, like an accident in the street. God may be the ultimate cause, but that does not mean that the earthquake dead had been naturally executed on official Divine instructions." Few, however, went as far as John Winthrop, the Boston astronomer and mathematician, in a talk in Harvard Chapel, shortly after the earthquake which shook Boston and much of New England on November 18, 1755. He saw earthquakes being of "real and standing advantage to the globe," as they opened the pores of the earth in much the same way that the plough breaks up clods of earth.

There was still a confusion between earthquakes and volcanoes, and they were assumed to share the same origins. But a certain Comte de Buffon who was at the height of his scientific fame in the 1770s, did detect a difference. In the preface to his *Natural History*, he demolished his predecessors' theories. "The whole of these hypotheses," he denounced, "are raised on unstable foundations; have given no light upon the subject, the ideas being unconnected, the facts confused, and the whole confounded with a mixture of physic and fable; and consequently have been adopted only by those who implicitly believe opinions without investigation, and who, incapable of distinguishing probability, are more impressed with the wonders of the marvelous than the relation of the truth." In later pages he divided earthquakes into two classes. The first were "occasioned by the action of subterranean fires and explosions of volcanoes," these were felt only to small distances and at the time the volcanoes were raging before the first eruption. The second, "very different to their effects and probably their causes too," were felt to vast distances and "shook long stretches of ground without the mediation of any new volcano or eruption." Buffon was ahead of his time. Nearly a century after the Frenchman had made his announcement, a scientist wrote, "An earthquake in a non-volcanic region may in fact be viewed as an uncompleted effort to establish a volcano." Even then, earthquakes were often stated as being the cause of volcanoes, or, more commonly, the volcano was the cause of the earthquake. There was considerable confusion between cause and effect. The classic case concerned a tribe, the Brutii, which lived in southern Italy in Roman days in an area later called "The Burnt Country." These worthies were renowned for their melancholy mien. But what observers could never satisfy themselves upon was whether they were of gloomy countenance because of the many earthquakes which ravaged the region – and this despite frequent human sacrifices which seemed to do little to abate the scourge – or if their doleful expressions actually encouraged the earthquakes which killed their people and destroyed their houses.

But to the ordinary person the earthquake remained a complete and unfathomable mystery and he would have been the first to support one authority who with resounding finality declared, "The causes of earthquakes are still hidden in obscurity, and probably will ever remain so, as these violent convulsions originate at depths far below the realms of human observation."

Theories of all sorts abounded as geological thinking progressed. The ancients had viewed mountains as the bones of body earth, the rivers its veins, hills as warts despoiling the "face" of earth and the tides caused by the pumping of some earthly blood by a "heart" hidden somewhere within it. Now, one man saw the mountain chains like a string of balls which were more or less elastic. A mass of inflammable material pent up in the bowels of these chains would be transmitted with immense velocity and activity, as it "stalked round the globe." Another put forward the hypothesis to account for the recent Lisbon disaster that Lisbon and Seville were connected by an "earthquake track," until it was pointed out to him that this was not supported in history as the two cities rarely suffered earthquakes simultaneously. Another theory proposed was that remarkable and highly abnormal accumulations of ice in the Polar regions had caused a deflection in the Gulf Stream. This drastic disruption in the normal state of affairs had caused considerable climatic changes and an alteration in the ocean bed. The consequent rush of cold water would account for the disappearance of the sardine during the year 1755.

Fanciful and extraordinary as they seem now, these were at least semi-scientific attempts to unravel the mystery of earthquakes. Rational thinking and analysis – although often suspect and faulty – had overtaken superstition and the supernatural, and informed the first efforts at developing a science which we now call seismology. Slowly, sometimes eccentrically, glimmerings of what we can recognize as light were beginning to emerge through the fog of ancient belief and strange theory.

A certain Dr. Robert Hooke in 1675 had postulated that there were as many earthquakes in the parts of the earth under the ocean as in the parts under dry land, and he conceived the idea that shells found on top of mountains were due to earthquakes which "have turned plains into mountains, and mountains into plains, seas into land, and land into seas, made rivers where there were none before, and swallowed up others that formerly were."

Then in 1760, an Englishman, John Michell, declared that "earthquakes were waves set up by the shifting masses of rock miles below the surface." The first tremors of modern earthquake theory and knowledge were beginning to make themselves felt on scientific minds. Michell went on to say that "the motion of the earth in earthquakes is partly tremulous and partly propagated by waves which succeed one another" and he estimated that the earthquake waves after the Lisbon earthquake had traveled outward at twelve hundred miles per hour (1,932 km per hour).

The earliest known government or private enquiry into the phenomenon of the earthquake was set up in China in the year A.D. 132. It came about due to the industry and vigilance of one man Chōkō (also called Chang Heng according to some reports). A translated account reads: "In the first year of Yoka (A.D. 136) a Chinese called Chōkō invented an instrument for indicating earthquakes. It consisted of a spherically formed copper vessel, the diameter of which was eight feet (2.4 m). In form it resembled a

Chōkō's Seismoscope. The first known seismoscope. When an earthquake took place a ball was dislodged from the dragon's mouth and fell into the frog's mouth below.

wine bottle, covered at its top. Its outer part was ornamented by the figures of different kinds of birds and animals, and other lettering. In the inner part of this instrument a column was so suspended that it can move in eight directions. Also, inside the bottle is an arrangement by which some record of an earthquake is made according to the movement of the pillar. On the outside of the bottle there were eight dragon heads, each holding a ball in its mouth. Underneath the heads were eight frogs so placed that they appear to watch the dragon's face, so that they are ready to receive the ball if it should be dropped. All the arrangements which cause the pillar to knock the ball out of the dragon's mouth are well hidden inside the bottle.

"When an earthquake occurs, and the bottle is shaken, the dragon instantly drops the ball, and the frog which receives it vibrates vigorously; anyone watching this instrument can easily observe earthquakes.

"Once upon a time a dragon dropped its ball without any earthquake being observed, and the people therefore thought the instrument of no use, but after two or three days a notice came saying that an earthquake had taken place at Rosei. Hearing of this, those who doubted the use of this instrument began to believe in it again. After this ingenious instrument had been invented by Chōkō, the Chinese government wisely appointed a secretary to make observations on earthquakes."

The earthquake indicated by Chōkō's instrument was pure coincidence as the device was not nearly sensitive enough to act as a seismoscope, but as late as the ninth century, the same principle for indicating earthquakes was in use. Some authorities employed bowls of water, some used mercury where the slightest tremor would be shown as ripples on the surface. The Reverend S. Chandler writing after the Lisbon quake, suggests that a great spherical bowl three to four foot (0.9–1.2 m) in diameter be used. The inside of this massive receptical was to be dusted over with "barber's puff," and then the whole very gently filled with water. This instrument was condemned by others as being "ridiculous and utterly impracticable."

A variant of the bowl was a circular trough of wood, with notches cut in the edge and filled with mercury. The earthquake would, in theory, dislodge the mercury and the particular notch which flooded would indicate the direction of the tremor. One of the problems of this type of seismoscope, as they came to be called, was that the movements on the water or colored liquid or mercury might be so slight that they could hardly be determined by the naked eye. To overcome this problem, small ships with high masts were set floating on the liquid and the motion of the masts then noted.

The unwieldiness of such primitive seismoscopes was one of their greatest disadvantages, so one ingenious man of science invented tubes of mercury whose ends were turned up and small floats of iron set adrift on the quicksilver. Gradually, as these devices and others were perfected, it became possible to detect earthquakes. These efforts were still a long way from true scientific earthquake study, but the early chapters of the story of

Cacciatore's Seismoscope. A number of devices were invented for detecting earthquakes; most used bowls of vary- ing size full of water, colored liquid or mercury. This one was made of wood.

Crown Copyright, Science Museum, London

seismology are very largely associated with the search for a suitable recorder of earthquakes.

One of the first to study the varying effects of earthquakes in relation to their apparent source of origin was Sir William Hamilton, who in 1764 was appointed British envoy at the court of the king of Naples. Although a noted observer of his day of natural phenomena and a member of the august Royal Society, he is best remembered as the cuckolded husband of Emma Hamilton, mistress of Admiral Horatio Nelson, Britain's greatest sea hero. Hamilton spent much time studying the volcanic outcrops in the region and was at hand during the mighty eruptions of Vesuvius in 1776 and 1777. When a catastrophic earthquake struck Calabria in 1783, he was quickly on the scene. His assessment that the "present earthquakes are occasioned by the operation of a volcano, the seat of which seems to be deep," was in accord with popular theories. Of greater significance in the history of seismology, he also noted in a report to the Royal Society the varying degrees of damage he observed as he traveled over the stricken area. He found that "all the towns and villages have been utterly ruined, and the spots where the greatest mortality has happened and most visible alteration of the face of the earth," occurred twenty-two miles (35.4 km) from where he reckoned the source of the quake had been. At seventy-two miles (116 km) on the other hand, he observed, "I plainly observed a gradation in the damage done to the buildings, as also in the degree of mortality, in proportion as the countries were more or less distant from this supposed centre of the evil."

The Calabrian earthquake of 1783, and its subsequent aftershocks which continued for several years, resulted in the most thorough assessment and report to date by the Neapolitan Academy of Sciences and Fine Letters. This recorded in detail the effect on the country and general terrain, describing the human suffering and epidemics which followed the succession of tremors, and noting the total want of pattern or order in the aftershocks. It also gave rise to a document by Domenico Pignataro which classified damage in what was the first scale of intensity. Other men of science examined the evidence of the Calabrian quake, and scientifically speaking, it became a milestone in the study of seismology.

There was little advance, however, in the science for the next half century. A number of men produced catalogs of earthquakes, enumerating those recorded or mentioned back into the dim mists of time, but for the most part they were bare lists. Early history was highly inaccurate and civil wars and other disturbances tended to interrupt the flow of observations while legends had a habit of coalescing. Nevertheless, from these rudimentary catalogs it was

In 1783, a violent earthquake shook Calabria in southern Italy. The town of Reggio was badly damaged.

British Museum

An engineer studies earthquake damage. Earthquake effects are shown on a monument in Padula, south Italy, after the great Neapolitan earthquake of 1857, the study of which led to the publishing of the first book on observational seismology, by Robert Mallet. British Library

possible to tell which were the most earthquake-prone areas in the world, and practicable to make rough estimates at the relative frequency of earthquakes in different countries.

Not however until the early 1850s did the first true seismologist, as we would recognize the term, appear on the scene. He was an Irishman, Robert Mallet.

Mallet was born in Dublin in 1810, and after taking a degree at Trinity College, Dublin he went into his father's small engineering factory. He remained an engineer all his life, and was responsible for a number of bridges over the River Shannon and many early central heating plants, ventilating apparatus and hydraulic rams. His designs for the great spans of railway station roofs were famous, and he rebuilt the lighthouse on the Fastnet

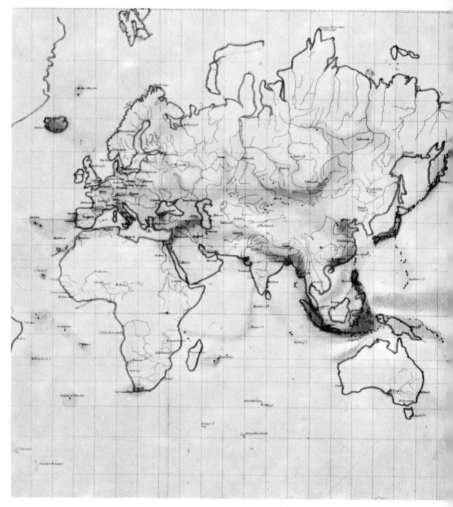

Mallet's study of earthquakes enabled him to produce a seismographic map of the world in 1857. The shaded areas indicate seismic zones.

Rock off the southern coast of Ireland, as well as constructing heavy pieces of artillery and mortars. But it is for his assessment and work on what became known as the Neapolitan Earthquake of 1857, that he is best known.

With care and diligence he set about examining the results of the Naples earthquake. He was, in effect, carrying out the suggestion of David Milne, a noted amateur geologist (afterward David Milne Home), who had predicted "If instruments could be invented which at different places would indicate, not merely the relative intensity of the shocks, but the direction in which they acted on bodies, means would be obtained of determining the point in the earth's interior from which the shocks originated." Mallet, for the time being, was using the oldest instruments in the world: his eyes, a compass and a measuring stick. By calculating the direction of the cracks in walls, the fall of columns and pillars, and the projection of fallen masonry he was able to

Professor N.N. Ambraseys

determine the epicenter – the point on the surface above the seismic focus. By measuring the angle of emergence he was also able to assess how deep was the focus, and by joining on a plan those points where the intensity appeared to be the same he created what is now called an isoseismal map.

Mallet's *The Great Neapolitan Earthquake of 1857: the First Principles of Observational Seismology* which followed his investigation was a milestone in the evolution of the science. As a result of his study, he concluded that an earthquake was due to the "sudden flexure and constraint of the elastic materials forming a portion of the earth's crust, or by their giving way and becoming fractured." He foresaw that it was on the sea bottom where it would seem to be "the most likely state of things to give rise to frequent and sudden local elevations or even submarine eruptions of molten matter."

Mallet also carried out a number of experiments to determine the velocity of earth waves. By setting off charges of explosive in different soils and by measuring the result on bowls of mercury set at varying distances up to half a mile (0.8 km) away, he was able to calculate how quickly waves could travel through the ground.

He also expanded his predecessors' catalog of earthquakes but by making use of every authority he could find in the libraries of Europe, Mallet's list was far more comprehensive than any there had been before. Following from this he compiled a bibliography of earthquakes, a work which mentioned no fewer than seven thousand books and pamphlets dating from 1606 B.C. to A.D. 1850. And using the material he had collected Mallet drew up a seismic map of the world.

Mallet's chief claim to seismological fame was his monograph on the Neapolitan earthquake, the first in a long line of specific earthquake studies. His experiences have been echoed by many eminent successors: "When the observer," he wrote in his great work, "first enters upon one of those earthquake-shaken towns, he finds himself in the midst of utter confusion. The eye is bewildered by 'a city become a heap.' He wanders over masses of dislocated stone and mortar. Houses seem to have been precipitated to the ground in every direction of azimuth. There seems no governing law, nor any indication of a prevailing direction of overturning force. It is only by first gaining some commanding point, whence a general view over the whole field of ruin can be had, and observing its places of greatest and least destruction, and then by patient examination, compass in hand, of many details of over-throw, house by house and street by street, analysing each detail and comparing the results . . . at length we perceive, once for all, that this apparent confusion is but superficial."

Mallet had relied on his bowl of mercury for earthquake and earth wave calculations, but already more precise measuring instruments were being perfected. An Italian, Luigi Palmieri, director of the Vesuvius volcanological observatory, developed a seismograph which comprized a clock which stopped as soon as a tremor took place, and set in motion a recording drum.

By the 1860s seismology was an international science. Although seismology is a very young science – indeed in its modern guise it is less than one hundred years old, and as a truly international pursuit, considerably less than that – it was gaining pace rapidly.

The differing degrees of damage shown on isoseismal maps which were compiled during earthquake investigations, suggested that an international scale should be drawn up to which seismologists could refer. In the past, an earthquake was measured by the loss of life and by total damage caused. Pignataro had used four degrees of destruction to prepare his isoseismal map after the Calabrian quake. Mallet had also employed four zones for his Neapolitan earthquake. An earthquake catalog compiled by a Swiss and two Italians showed the degrees of damage by shading.

At first there were a number of different scales. Some were a purely local

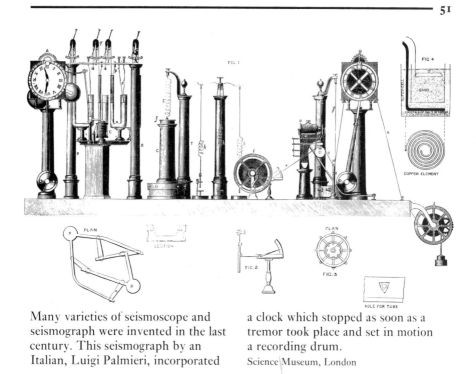

Many varieties of seismoscope and seismograph were invented in the last century. This seismograph by an Italian, Luigi Palmieri, incorporated a clock which stopped as soon as a tremor took place and set in motion a recording drum.

Science Museum, London

variety, such as one in Australia which included a degree of intensity compared to a horse rubbing itself against the veranda post; but even this was of more value than another which blandly said that the intensity concerned could "only be felt by the experienced observer" – whatever that meant! Gradually, from a large international field, the Mercalli, and subsequently Modified Mercalli scale we employ today, evolved which equates damage according to a scale (measurements on the Modified Mercalli scale, or MM for short are usually shown in Roman numerals) from I which is an intensity of tremor hardly detectable to human beings, through to XII which involves total damage. (See Appendix A.)

Seismology was also exercising the authorities. In many countries, commissions or committees were appointed by either governments or learned societies for the observation, recording and cataloging of earthquakes. The Swiss were one of the first nations to do so, while earthquakes in 1881 and 1883 in Italy led to the foundation of a body which produced a regular journal devoted to the "Science of Endogenous Forces of the Earth." Before this, one man, who has been called the father of seismology had made a remarkable impact on the study of earthquakes. This was John Milne.

Milne was born in Lancashire, England in 1850 and studied as a mining engineer. He was an inveterate traveler and before he was twenty-five had taken part in expeditions to places as far afield as Newfoundland and the Arabian desert. Then, in 1875 he was offered the post which was to monopo-

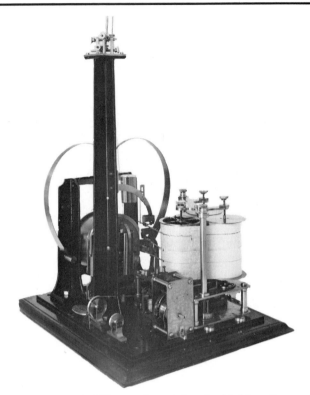

After his arrival in Japan, John Milne was responsible for the invention of a number of seismographs. This is one he produced with his colleague Gray.

Crown Copyright, Science Museum, London

| Modified Mercalli scale | II | III | IV | V |
|---|---|---|---|---|
| Chinese Classification | 1-2 | 3 | 4-5 | 6 |
| | | | | |
| Reaction of people and buildings. | Not felt by people generally. Just recordable by seismograph. | A few people indoors notice a slight vibration. | Sleeping persons wake. Hanging items like lamps swing. | Things indoors fall over. |

Many nations use the Modified Mercalli scale of earthquake damage, but some countries employ their own. This is the Chinese version.

lize his working life, as Professor of Geology and Mining at the Imperial College of Engineering in Tokyo. He hated the sea, and so he determined to travel overland to his new post. Accordingly, he set out across Europe and Russia, and eventually reached Japan eleven months later – to be almost immediately greeted by an earthquake.

For some time past the Japanese had been applying a good deal of study and analysis to their earthquakes and to this burgeoning interest Milne added his own considerable energies. An earthquake in 1880 near Yokohama prompted him to propose the creation of the Seismological Society of Japan, the first of its kind. Before he left Japan after twenty years at the Imperial University, there were seven hundred stations for observing earthquake phenomena across Japan.

Milne found two principal problems: the poor communications which prevailed throughout the great Japanese Empire, and the lack of a reliable instrument for measuring earthquakes.

The first he resolved by sending out bundles of postcards to all the outlying towns and cities, with instructions to the postal authorities to send back each week a card reporting on the number of earthquakes which had taken place during the previous seven days. In this way it was possible to create seismic maps, and isoseismal diagrams for all subsequent Japanese earthquakes.

The second, which involved the invention of a proper seismograph, was more complex. On his arrival he found that the Japanese were making use of magnetic seismometers which were inspired by the experiences of a Tokyo

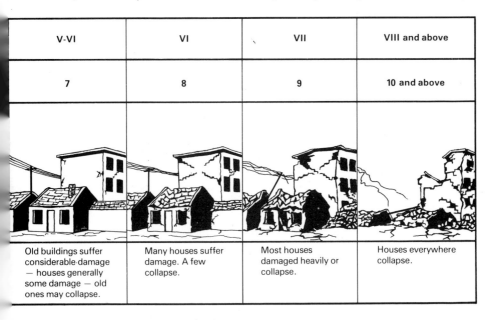

| V-VI | VI | VII | VIII and above |
|---|---|---|---|
| 7 | 8 | 9 | 10 and above |
| Old buildings suffer considerable damage — houses generally some damage — old ones may collapse. | Many houses suffer damage. A few collapse. | Most houses damaged heavily or collapse. | Houses everywhere collapse. |

spectacle maker. The spectacle maker had hung a magnet on his wall, with a large number of nails hanging from it. Imagine his surprise, when, shortly before an earthquake, all the nails suddenly fell off. Somehow, the magnet had temporarily lost its power. The magnetic instrument which was developed as a result of this observation was neither sensitive nor accurate. Milne and his colleagues, Gray and Ewing, set to constructing more precise earthquake measuring devices. The principal problem was how to produce a body which would remain stationary, and to all intents and purposes detached from the world around in order to record the relative movement of the ground on which it actually rested. They decided to make use of the mechanical principle of inertia – in essence the tendency of a heavy body to stay put. Thus the earliest seismometers, as these instruments were called, relied on using a freely swinging pendulum whose movements were marked by pin or pen on a revolving drum of smoked glass, and later paper. This instrument showed that when an earthquake struck and the ground beneath moved or vibrated, it did so in clearly recognizable periods of greater or lesser activity, in waves in fact. Milne also found that these waves were not only backward and forward as he had expected, but from side to side and even up and down. Early forms of the Milne seismographs employed three devices, one for each form of wave movement, although the up and down variety could only be measured by using a spring which jerked when affected. This was the general principle behind the early seismographs, and is the basic idea on which rests the designs of many modern instruments.

Complications arose because a pendulum once set in motion will continue to swing unless halted. A quake would set the pendulum swinging, and that initial jerk could be measured, but subsequent movement due to the pendulum rather than the shock had to be eliminated. Any swinging body has a natural period of oscillation, and if this coincided with the period of the earthquake wave then a greatly magnified reading would result. The "damping" of the pendulum caused a number of headaches. Over the years, refinements and improvements have occurred both in the actual means of detecting an earthquake and in its method of recording, but the honor of providing the initial impetus to the accurate recording of earthquakes belongs to John Milne.

In 1895, after twenty years in Japan and having seen the establishment of a Chair of Seismology at the Imperial University, and an Earthquake Investigating Committee established by Imperial ordinance, Milne went back to England. Before leaving he had been presented with the Order of the Rising Sun – an honor rarely accorded to a foreigner.

On his return, Milne bought a small property on the Isle of Wight, off the southern coast of England, and there set up what was to become the center of a worldwide seismological network. Using the material he collected he published a series of maps of worldwide earthquake distribution, from which it was possible to determine the principal areas of seismic activity.

In his small house at Shide in the Isle of Wight, Milne set up his first seismographs in the stables, which had solid foundations on the local chalk, perfect for his purposes. Later, when he decided to set up another apparatus away from his house, he was able to persuade the local yacht club to let him use their grounds.

In due time the new seismograph was established, and each day Milne or an assistant would inspect the smoked drum on which any seismic activity would be recorded. For days there was not so much as a quiver to be seen. Then one evening he paid his usual call, and to his astonishment discovered that a little time previously the needle had nearly shot off the drum, indicating violent tremors. Milne hurried back eagerly to see what the other seismographs had recorded. He was more than a little puzzled to find that they showed nothing at all; and there were no indications from other stations in his network.

The yacht club seismograph showed no further movement after that one burst of activity until, on the same day the following week and at the same time, the needle jerked violently. Once more there was no indication on his other instruments, and no postcards or telegrams arrived to report a shattering earthquake somewhere in the world.

The mystery remained complete. At precisely the same time each week the strange, violent tremors were regularly repeated. Milne soon came to the conclusion that whatever was causing these astonishing movements must be a purely local phenomenon. But there was no quarry blasting in progress; the Royal Navy was not conducting torpedo or gunnery practice in the waters of the Solent; and traffic in the local town could be ruled out. At length, after the most detailed and thorough examination, it was discovered that the movements took place only when the butler and the housekeeper at the yacht club had their afternoon off together!

The work in Japan of Milne and his colleagues, both Japanese and European, set the course of seismology on the right track at last, but there remained confusion in the distinction between an earthquake cause and effect. Then in 1891 a Japanese seismologist, Professor B. Koto, after careful study of what was called the Mino-Owari earthquake noted, "It can be confidently asserted that the sudden faulting was the actual cause (and not the effect) of the earthquake." This pronouncement was the start of common acceptance that fractures, faults, and fissures were the actual mechanism of the earthquake and not its results, and was the basis of the development of the modern science of seismology.

Ironically man's enthusiasm for blowing himself up has led to the serious establishment of seismology as a lifesaving science. Not until military necessity required a careful measurement and monitoring of nuclear explosions was any nation prepared to devote enough money and effort into a thorough and systematic probing of the mysteries of the earth. The Nuclear

Test Detection Program in which over one hundred seismographs were set up on a global scale provided the base work for the Worldwide Standardized Seismograph Network (WWSSN) which spans the globe today. It comprises 123 stations in most countries, from the South Pole to the Arctic, with the exception of the Eastern Bloc and China.

Early seismologists believed that energy from an underground tumult like an earthquake spread out evenly from the central focus, but it has been

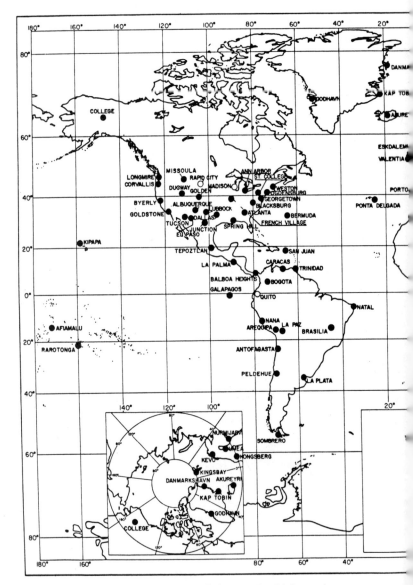

Seismology is international. A map showing the many stations of the Worldwide Standardized Seismograph Network (WWSSN) which monitor earthquakes across the world.

NEIS

discovered that this is far from the case. Earthquakes generate many types of waves in complex patterns. Some penetrate the earth and come to the surface in the same state, or slightly distorted. Others are reflected, or refracted, bent by something or some zone of different density within the earth itself; some kinds travel round the circumference of the world and do not penetrate at all.

The simplest waves are the primary (P waves), and the secondary

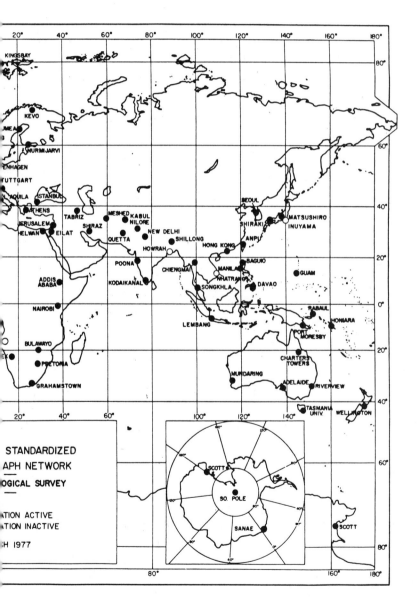

(S waves). P waves are compressional waves which exert a pull-push force, as when a stick or rod is given a sharp tap. The force or vibration created will travel up the rod, but will not bend the rod itself. The S wave on the other hand – normally known as the shear wave – is a transverse wave like those produced in a side-to-side jerk given to a length of rope. This wave can be seen traveling up the length of the rope until it arrives at the further end. These, in greatly simplified examples, are the principal waves exerted by an earthquake.

P and S waves do not travel at the same speed, and these speeds vary with the substance through which the waves are passing. Broadly speaking, a P wave travels faster than an S wave. The P wave travels at about 5 miles (8 km) per second, the S wave at only $2\frac{3}{4}$ miles (4.5 km) per second. Thus, inevitably, the P wave arrives first. The further an observer is from the focus of the earthquake the longer the gap between the arrival of the P and the following S wave. If the earthquake is nearby, then, except to the most sensitive instruments, the P and S wave will appear to arrive simultaneously. The advance P wave gives the seismologist warning of the much greater S wave to follow. The length of the time between the arrival of the P and the S wave gives an indication of the distance an earthquake is away from an observer. By using three or more stations recording the direction from which the shock came, it is possible to pinpoint where the earthquake occurred.

Recently, it has been found that the ratio of the speeds of the P and S waves varies before an earthquake. This is due, it is believed, to an alteration in the state of the underlying rocks, a condition known as dilatancy, which is closely linked to the squeezing effect on rock strata as earthquake strain is building up. Even in its early days as an earthquake precursor, this variation in the speeds of the P and S waves is already proving a promising field for accurate, credible, reliable earthquake prediction.

Although the use of an international scale of intensity, which defined the degree of destruction and required no measurement other than the evidence of the eye, was satisfactory up to a point, it was not a true reflection of the power of an earthquake, for the damage caused by say an intensity x earthquake in rural Turkey would be less than one of only intensity VII in the urban areas of Japan, where the material and human cost might well be colossal. The only correlation between earthquakes in Turkey or Japan, or anywhere else in the world must be measured in the energy emitted.

Dr. Charles Richter, the doyen of seismologists, who recently retired from the Californian Institute of Technology but is still very active in the seismological world, devised what we know as the Richter scale of measuring earthquake magnitude. At first the scale was intended to deal with Californian earthquakes only, but with the cooperation of Professor Beno Gutenberg – another name known far outside the realms of seismology and science – the scale was adapted to enable earthquakes to be classified worldwide. It is the Richter scale of magnitude which is in common use today, although some other nations have their own equivalents. It is what is termed an open-ended scale, implying that there is no upper limit to the amount of energy an earthquake might release, but in practice it is felt that any rock strata would have given way before the theoretical figure of 10.0 is reached on the Richter scale. The first scale was drawn up in 1935 and it stood untouched until slightly revised in 1977. (This revision adjusted the magnitude of a number of historic earthquakes; thus, the San Francisco earthquake of 1906, formerly considered one of 8.3 magnitude is now lowered to 7.9; the great Chilean quake of 1960, previously 8.6, is now looked on as having been a massive 9.5; while the Alaskan earthquake of 1964 is now thought to have been 9.2.)

The Richter scale which measures the vibrational energy of a shock is essentially a logarithmic one, that is to say each increase of a full figure is an increase of ten in the energy released. Thus a 7.5 quake is roughly ten times stronger than one of 6.5, and an 8.0 no less than one hundred times stronger than one of magnitude 6.0. If one considers that the atom bomb dropped on Hiroshima and Nagasaki was equivalent to a 5.5 quake, that in Chile registering 8.5 on the Richter scale was *one thousand* times stronger. But in calculating true energy released in an earthquake, other factors come into play and the difference is considerably greater.

It is difficult to equate intensity with magnitude as so many factors are involved – style of building, density of population, nature of the underlying soil and so on. A greater magnitude usually means a higher degree of damage, death and destruction, but this is by no means always the case, as a shallow shock may be felt over a comparatively small area and cause colossal destruction, whereas a deeper shock may occasion only moderate shaking over a much greater area and do little damage.

It has been through the study and measurement of ground waves, either natural waves produced by earthquakes, or artificial waves due to the explosion of a nuclear or non-nuclear device, that we owe our present knowledge of the earth's composition. By means of this "prospecting," as one eminent seismologist has called the process, it has been possible to determine the structure of the earth. It is now believed that at the center of this globe – this irregular ball 7,900 miles (12,719 km) in diameter revolving around a sun 92 million miles (148 million km) away – lie two cores which occupy roughly half the radius of earth.

The inner core, some 850 miles (1,370 km) in radius is a solid mass bound together by immense compressional forces, and is principally composed of iron, with traces of dissolved sulfur, silicon and other materials.

Surrounding this is the outer core. Rather larger, 1,242 miles (2,000 km) thick, this is in a semi-molten state and is also largely composed of iron. Within this band, and generated by movements and fluctuations of this semi-solid mass, it is believed lies the earth's magnetic field.

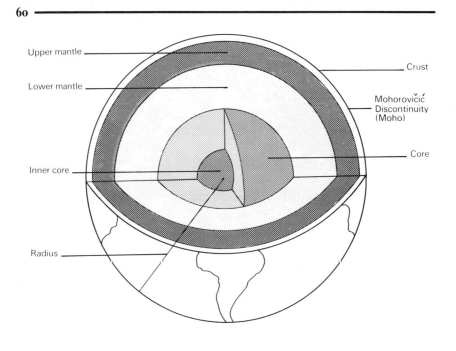

Upper mantle

Lower mantle

Inner core

Radius

Crust

Mohorovičić
Discontinuity
(Moho)

Core

The interior of the earth.

Around the outer core is the mantle which is 1,863 miles (3,000 km) thick. The mantle is subjected to immense pressure believed to be in the order of 11,000 tons per square inch, and is very hot.

The outer covering is known as the crust, and it was Darwin who predicted its existence. "A bad earthquake at once destroys our oldest associations," he wrote during his epic round-the-world voyage on the *Beagle*, "the earth, the very emblem of solidity, has moved beneath our feet like a thin crust over a fluid." What Darwin did not know is that the crust varies in thickness. In some places on the ocean floor it is as little as $3\frac{1}{2}$ miles (6 km) thick, at others, such as under some mountain ranges, it can be as much as 44 miles (70 km) deep; but for the most part the crust varies in depth between 18 and 30 miles (30–48 km).

The world may be compared to a softboiled egg: the core is the yolk; the solid mantle is the white, while the crust and upper portion of the mantle is the shell. This concept is not wholly new: in 1872 Benjamin Franklin proposed that the surface of the globe would be a shell, "swimming" on some inner fluid.

In 1910 a Yygoslavian seismologist called Mohorovičić, when studying an earthquake which had occurred in a valley in Croatia, was surprised to discover that seismographs near the epicenter did not show simple phases of P and S waves, but had secondary ones following later. It was almost as if waves when passing through the earth had rebounded off some layer below the earth's crust, and, even more strangely, were accelerating as they did so. This was the discovery of what became known as the Mohorovičić Discontinuity. Efforts have been made to bore down through the crust to the Mohorovičić Discontinuity. In the Upper Mantle Project, a barge was moored off the Californian coast in the San Diego trough where the ocean is 3,000 feet (900 m) deep – a project irreverently known as Mohole – and probing began. After a wealth of administrative and other difficulties, the project was discontinued in 1966 with comparatively meager results. More promising is a Russian experiment which began in May 1978 in the Republic of Azerbaijan to bore over a spot where the crust was 9 miles (15 km) thick. As the deepest known borehole (in Washita County, Oklahoma) is only a little over 6 miles (9.6 km) down, the immensity of the project is awesome.

The crust is not continuous. Some areas are weaker or thinner than others. Occasionally some mighty strain places undue pressure on a certain point, and when this happens a slippage may occur between two rock faces. Sometimes this slippage may be caused by drought, or excessive rain, or undermining, either natural or artificial. When it occurs geologically it is known as faulting.

Geological faults appear in different guises. Some are only in one plane; some are in several planes. These fractures are brought about by immense pressure exerted on a rock, which is so extreme that the rock can stand no more. Some rocks are more brittle than others; some can bend elastically to a greater degree than others; but every substance has its breaking point. When rock reaches this point, the effect may be catastrophic, and it is the effort to re-establish an equilibrium afterward which causes an earthquake.

Shortly after the San Francisco quake of 1906 an American geologist, Harry Fielding Reid, investigated the geological aftermath. He noticed that in places a displacement of nearly twenty feet (6 m) had occurred on certain

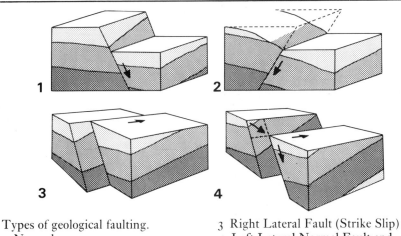

Types of geological faulting.
1 Normal
2 Reverse

3 Right Lateral Fault (Strike Slip)
4 Left Lateral Normal Fault and Left Oblique Normal Fault

parts of the San Andreas fault which runs under San Francisco, and he propounded the theory that strain had been building up for ages and had found release in the recent quake. As he put it: "It is impossible for rock to rupture without first being subjected to elastic strains greater than it can endure. We conclude that the crust in many parts of the earth is being *slowly* displaced, and the difference between displacements in neighboring regions sets up elastic strains, which may become larger than the rock can endure. A rupture then takes place, and the strained rock rebounds under its own elastic stresses, until the strain is largely or wholly relieved. In the majority of cases, the elastic rebound on opposite sides of the fault are in opposite directions."

This is known as the elastic rebound theory. Its significance lies in the concept of earthquakes being the product not of a sudden process, but of a gradual one as the continuing strain on rocks builds up over the passage of years. A lesser phenomenon, but one which can cause considerable damage in a building, is called creep, and symptomises the very gradual readjustment of a fault. A building sited immediately over a fault and subject to creep will gradually be damaged or destroyed. Scientists are in several minds over whether creep can lessen the potential impact of an earthquake by slowly relieving strain, or whether excessive creep presages the coming of a sizeable tremor.

Fault creep. This sidewalk in California has become distorted through the gradual shift of part of the earth's crust.

As the frontiers of the known world extended and maps of increasing accuracy and reliability came to be produced, a remarkable phenomenon began to emerge. It was noticed that there was an amazing similarity in the shapes of some continents. In particular it was as though someone with a knife had carved between Africa and South America – the bulge of Brazil would fit almost exactly with the Gulf of Guinea, the armpit of Africa, and other similarities were not hard to find. This was the birth of what has now come to be called global tectonics (from the Greek *tekton*, a builder).

Over the years a number of people commented on the indications that once South America and Africa must have been one great land mass, until in 1910 a German meteorologist and astronomer, Alfred Wegener, put forward a theory considered preposterous at the time. Wegener suggested that at one time the earth, 200 or so million years ago, consisted of only one continent, which he called Pangaea (all lands) and one ocean, Panthalassa (all seas). Eventually, for reasons which Wegener could not explain, this mass of land broke up in mesozoic times – about 150 million years ago – and started to move; firstly into north-south divisions, and then into east-west ones. He called the process continental drift.

Thus Pangaea broke into a northern half, Laurasia, and a southern one, Gondwana; and subsequently the two halves broke transversely. This led to Laurasia splitting into what is now Asia and North America; while Gondwana broke into the other continents of the southern hemisphere – Antarctica, Australia and New Zealand, Africa and South America. Another portion of Gondwana came adrift and made northwards to create the Indian sub-continent, divided from the mass of Laurasia by the Himalayas.

The Wegener theory was too fanciful for many, and at the existing level of scientific knowledge it could not be proved. Wegener was roundly condemned. After all he was not a geologist at all, and he dared to "take liberties with our globe", as one geologist wrote in deep disgust. The whole proposition was damned as unscientific and it was pointed out by critics that the theory was of the "footloose" type, in which the author was blind to every fact that told against his conceptions.

The theory of continental drift was all but forgotten, when the discovery of submarine mountain ranges, made scientists disinter the Wegener concept. The more they looked at it, the more they saw it as solving a number of hitherto unexplained phenomena and relationships. Not only was it attractive and plausible, it was the only tenable theory.

Once the hypothesis was generally accepted, more and more evidence started to come to light broadly confirming Wegener's ideas. The German had written, "It is just as if we were to refit the torn pieces of newspapers by matching its edges and then check whether the lines of print run smoothly across. If they do, there is nothing left but to conclude that the pieces were in fact joined this way." The "lines of print" were fossil remains, geological structure and magnetism in rocks and they showed that there was evidence

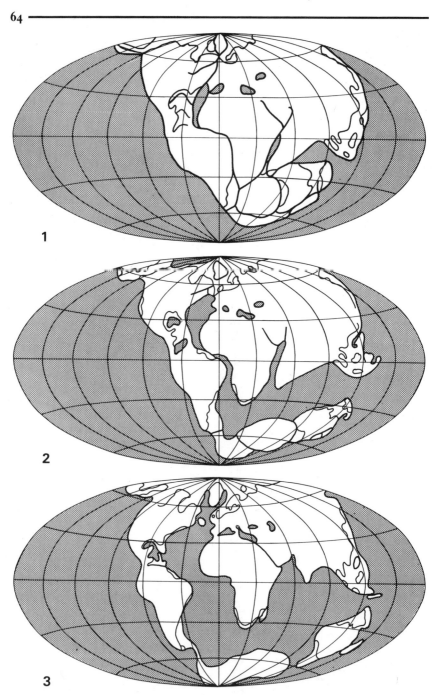

1

2

3

Diagrams illustrating Wegener's theory of continental drift.

1 270 million years ago, the continents were united in a single block called Pangaea.
2 150 million years ago, Pangaea started to divide. North America and Europe were still united. It is now believed that North and South America were apart at this stage.
3 1 million years ago, the continents were beginning to assume the shapes and positions we know today.

The continuation of the great East African Rift Valley – the Red Sea, the Gulf of Aqaba (seen running north-west from the right center of the picture) to the Dead Sea and the Sea of Galilee can be seen like a great scar across the earth. (A picture taken from the Gemini XI space mission, September, 1966).

of the same origin on either side of the Atlantic Ocean. Indeed, geologically speaking, certain tracts of South America were indistinguishable from areas of South West Africa. The Cape fold belt of South Africa finds a continuation in the Buenos Aires province of Argentina, and other similarities could also be found. It was known for some time that certain fossils had their counterparts directly across the ocean, but in the past it had been thought that land bridges had existed. The Wegener theory turned the old ideas upside down.

The impact of the theories of plate tectonics and continental drift was immense and was the great breakthrough that the earth sciences had needed for so long. Now at last it was possible to see how the world was constructed and had been shaped in the past. It was realized that the surface of the world,

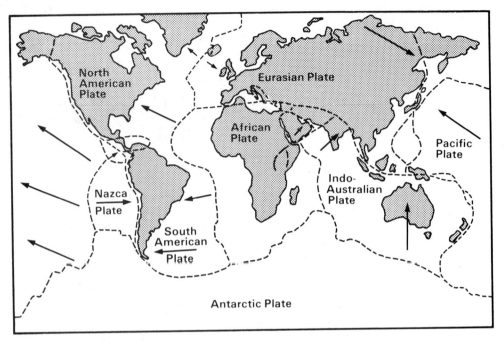

Tectonic plates of the earth.

sea and land, comprized a collection of plates floating on the bulk of the earth below.

The continents can be loosely described therefore as land masses sliding on a semi-molten bed. This could explain the existence of shores and ocean shelving, of faults and broad fissures, of the existence of the Red Sea, the Rift Valley and other geophysical divisions which are clear to the ordinary person and geologist alike, but it could not explain the constant growing strains of the earth. How could the stresses and strains beneath the crust cause restlessness at the earth's surface? The solution seemed to lie in the depths of the oceans.

The development of acoustics in World War II made it possible for the first time to accurately map the ocean floors. As oceanography advanced, it became apparent that beneath the seas lies an immense mountain chain, a snake-like ridge, with numerous lesser folds and hillocks, which stretches for 40,000 miles (64,400 km). Down the center of the mid–Atlantic ridge is a deep and steep cleft, very like the Rift Valley in East Africa. Magnetometers were trailed behind survey vessels and it was discovered, to everyone's surprise, that there appeared to be stripes of magnetic similarity running parallel to the underwater ridges. It has been known for some time that the earth's magnetic field "flips" diametrically 180 degrees every hundred thousand years or so. Two Cambridge geophysicists, Vine and Matthews, noticed that what was being revealed were stripes of magnetic activity, those on one side of the rift being a mirror image of those on the other side, and further, that those nearest the rift were in geological terms younger than

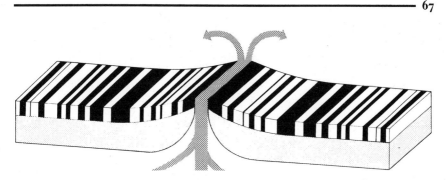

Molten magma welling from beneath the earth's crust passes through the central rift and hardens. As the process continues – as it has continued for millions of years – the magnetic "signature" of each long convulsion is "stamped" on the ocean floor. Alternating stripes then record the "flips" in the prevailing magnetic field of the earth which are known to take place every 100,000 years or so.

those beyond. They put forward the hypothesis that what caused these stripes was fresh magma welling up from the underlying core, as though squeezed from a toothpaste tube, and forcing itself through a crack in the earth's crust between two continental plates. As the magma was forced upward, it cooled and solidified to create the submarine mountains – and as this was happening, constant strains were imposed on the cracks between the plates as they were inexorably forced outward.

The picture now emerging was of great floating plates free to slide on a lower slippery surface, being pushed apart as molten magma was forced between them from below. The sea floor was literally spreading. But what was happening on the outer fringes of the plates as the process continued? In places a plate might be pushed under another; in other places the continental fringes might be buckling as one continent met another; occasionally, one plate might slide past another.

The plates are never still, and are free to move and jostle. In the Atlantic Ocean the plates are wide apart and separating at a rate of $1\frac{1}{2}$ inches (3 cm) a year moving Europe away from North America. In South America, the plates are crushing in on one another, and the Pacific Ocean floor is sliding under the continent. The plates on either side of the notorious San Andreas fault are moving beside one another, while the Pacific Plate near California is moving an average of two inches (5.08 cm) a year to the northwest. Los Angeles, which rests on the Pacific Plate and lies west of the San Andreas fault, is approaching San Francisco at a rate of one foot (0.3 m) every six years – it took a leap of no less than ten feet (3 m) during and after the great Californian earthquake of 1906 which devastated the state capital.

Elsewhere, India has been heading north for aeons and is still continuing to do so, buckling and doubling back on itself to create the Himalayas as it meets the main Asian land mass and in the process compressing Tibet;

Seismological equipment in the field. This installation is designed to monitor local earthquakes in New Mexico.

USGS

simultaneously, China is edging eastward. In the Middle East, the Red Sea is opening up. This in turn is pushing Arabia northward to squeeze Iran to the east and Turkey to the west. The effect is like a pair of scissors.

It is on the margins of the restless plates of the world that the great seismic areas of the world are located and most of the mineral deposits, but the fact that rogue earthquakes occur from time to time outside these seismic areas, shows just how incomplete is our knowledge of the world on which we live.

Part of the complex of equipment which monitors earthquakes worldwide from the National Earthquake Information Service in Golden, Colorado.

Recently it has been suggested that another supercontinent in addition to the Pangaea of Alfred Wegener existed 225 million years ago. This has been called Pacifica and is believed to have been situated broadly across the South Pacific and New Zealand. Gradually, it is supposed, this continent disintegrated, to collide with the continents around the Pacific and create the South American Andes, and the Rockies. This theory would satisfy the curiosity of botanists and zoologists who have long been puzzled at the connection between certain families of plants and animals on either side of the Pacific.

For the most part, the process of squeezing or intrusion by the magma between the plates is a placid and slow one, but occasionally the magma may behave in a less than ordered manner. When this occurs, a volcano results; occasionally the creation of a new island. As Humboldt, the noted nineteenth century geographer and traveler noted: "Molten masses, issuing from unknown depths, flow in narrow streams down the declivities of mountains, sometimes with an impetuous, and sometimes with a slow and gentle motion, until the fiery subterranean fount is dry." It is interesting to note that Darwin, from the evidence of a chain of volcanic eruptions which took place in Chile when he was there concluded that a "vast leak of melted matter . . . is spread out beneath a mere crust of solid land."

A volcano starts as a vent from which gas and ash escapes. Magma may escape in the form of lava, and occasionally it is forcibly ejected and the volcano erupts. The magma is not very hot – just enough to keep it molten – and when exposed to air it soon solidifies to make the characteristic cone formation of a volcano. The whole process completely mystified our ancestors. It was announced by one "scientist" in the middle of the eighteenth century, that "volcanoes begin first to kindle near the surface or top of the mountains and not in the caverns in the lower parts of them." Another likened a volcano to an immense cannon. In Iceland the groanings of a volcano are attributed to the cries of the damned and its eruption is the desperation and ungovernable fury of devils and tormented spirits.

A connection between earthquake and volcano has long been sought by man. The Owens Valley earthquake in California, March 1872 during which one observer graphically reported the "whole country turned topsy-turvy" also caused a curious phenomenon at the Black Rock, "which is supposed to be an extinct volcano." Here it was noted that "flashes of light were seen to issue from the top of the mountain, and streams of fire ran down its sides."

The connection developed from the practicable and possible to the mere fanciful. At Antioch in Asia Minor in the same year there were no volcanic phenomena observed, but one reverend gentleman did notice a nearby hill of "peculiar conical form which is very suggestive of an ancient volcano." In the absence of any recent or ancient volcano the writer then went on to describe an earthquake at Accra on the Gold Coast (Ghana), but finally decided the cause of the "unwonted atmospheric disturbance" was a fierce hurricane which wrecked every vessel but one at Zanzibar – on the other side of Africa! However, all these observations, and imaginings, led him to suspect that in some way or other these volcanic countries must be connected underground and happen to be situated over subterranean furnaces – places where "access to the exterior is more easy for the molten matter which lies underneath a great part, perhaps all, of the earth's crust." The reason for the extinction, however, of some volcanoes, was the dearth of water "to rouse them into action."

Although it is now generally accepted that the global tectonic plate system and the spreading of the ocean floor are the basic causes of earthquakes, there are those who remain unconvinced, and others who are not satisfied that this is the whole solution. Many believe that the celestial bodies exert some influence, if not in triggering earthquakes, at least in triggering the trigger. The Babylonians believed that earthquakes took place when the earth came too near the sun, and that Saturn, Jupiter and Mars were responsible. Others stated, in their earnest and frantic search for explanations and untiring efforts to find a plausible link, that earthquakes were more likely to occur in spring and autumn, during a drought or rainy period, and probably when there was no wind. A gentleman by the name of Thomas Twynne wrote after the 1580 earthquake in England: "The efficient causes of the Earthquakes are three," he wrote, "to wyt, the Sun, the other six Planets, and a Spirite or Breath included wythin the bowelles of the Earth," especially when the latter was "hot and Drie." The eclipse of the moon was also thought to bring on earthquakes – indeed, it is interesting to note that as recently as the San Fernando Earthquake of 1971 explanations were offered that the moon was a definite factor in triggering the quake.

In the constant search for some pattern in earthquake behavior scientists ransacked old records, but earthquakes were found to occur in all seasons, at night as well as in the day and "under all varieties of constellation indifferently." The moon was different. If the moon affects the tides in the oceans why not also the fluids within the earth itself? Rudolf Falb in the year 1875, was quite clear that the relative positions of sun and moon did affect earthquakes – and thus rendered them wholly predictable. He had gained great prestige when he had correctly forecast an earthquake in Belluno in North Italy in 1873, and an eruption of Mount Etna the following year. For good measure he also predicted that there would be a great flood over the earth in the year A.D. 6400!

A relationship with the moon and tides has long been considered a possible source of earthquake knowledge. Some calculated that earthquakes were more frequent at the new or full moon, and when the moon is nearest the earth (perigee) than when it is further away (apogee). In a diary written as long ago as 1618 a visitor to Japan noted: "And as we retorned, about ten aclock, hapned a greate earthquake, which caused many people to run out of their howses. And about the lyke hower the night following hapned an other, this countrey being much subject to them. And that which is comunely markd, they allwais hapen at hie water (or full sea); to it is thought it chauseth per reason is much wind blowen into hollow caves under ground at a loe water, and the sea flowing in after, and stoping the passage out, causeth these earthquakes, to fynd passage or vent for the wind shut up."

A further phenomenon which has long interested geophysicists is what is known as the Chandler Wobble – the peculiar deviation of the earth from the true north-south axis. One theory has been that seismic activity triggered this wavering. It has now been proposed that something else, perhaps massive movements of the atmosphere, sets the whole globe wobbling, and this in turn triggers earthquake activity. But this as yet is still in the realms of speculation.

# 3
# Earthquake Country

MAPS ILLUSTRATING the volcanic and earthquake regions of the world demonstrate clearly the immense power and elemental forces of nature which are lying beneath our feet. For this earth of ours is far from the solid sphere it appears. Earth is still, according to the geophysicists and astronomers, a "living" planet, and one subject to all the stresses and strains of puberty and adolescence.

It has been calculated that every year there will be two earthquakes of 7.7 magnitude or greater; seventeen between 7.7 and 7.0; one hundred between 6.0 and 7.0; and no less than fifty thousand between 3.0 and 4.0.

Nearly 90 percent of these earthquakes will take place in two long, narrow zones. The first zone completely girdles the Pacific Ocean and is known colloquially as the Ring of Fire; the second sweeps in a great majestic arc from the Sunda archipelago in the East Indies upward to embrace the Himalayas, the Hindu Kush, Iran, the Caucasus, Turkey, the Aegean area, the Carpathians, the Alps, Apennines and the Atlas Mountains.

Earthquakes vary in depth. Most are what are known as shallow foci earthquakes – that is with their focus less than 44 miles (70 km) deep. The deeper foci earthquakes, those whose origins lie in excess of 186 miles (300 km) and down to 435 miles (700 km) have a less extensive range than those of the Pacific plate – south of Japan and extending in a loop through the East Indies and the South Seas.

There are three main types of region prone to earthquakes; the mid–ocean ridges which produce principally shallow earthquakes; areas where one plate may be thrusting under another, such as on the Marianas Trench off Japan, or under the South American land mass – earthquakes here have a tendency to be of a magnitude of 5.0 or 6.0 and often greater – and a third where lateral movement by neighboring plates is taking place, such as on the San Andreas fault in California.

Extensive areas of the planet are referred to as "stable" zones, but even here earthquakes can and do occur. In the words of an eighteenth-century man learned in the affairs of nature, "We err if we believe any part of this Earth excused and free from this Hazard. All countries of the world are

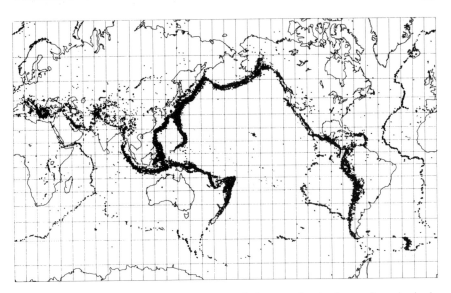

A seismic map of the world. Each dot represents an earthquake and the whole map clearly shows the principal earthquake zones of the world. NEIS

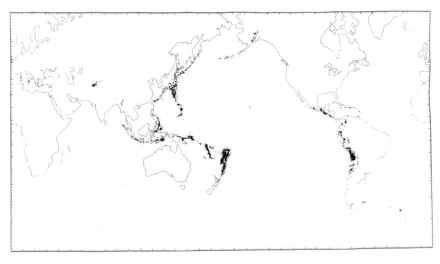

The seismicity of the earth. Most of the deeper earthquakes occur along what is colloquially known as the "Ring of Fire" stretching from New Zealand around the Pacific Ocean.
Seismological Society of America

subject to these Convulsions, but most of all that are most mountainous."

Principally, the stable zones of the earth are associated with what geologists call shields, often formed of extremely ancient mountains, eroded down by wind, weather and time mainly in the centers of continents. Stable zones include Scandinavia, Greenland, Eastern Canada, parts of north-western Siberia and Russia, Arabia, the lower portions of the Indian sub-

Looking south over the South American side of the "Ring of Fire" there is an area characterized by deep and massive earthquakes. (A picture taken from the second Skylab mission in September, 1973). NASA

continent and Indo-China peninsula, almost all South America except the Andes region, the whole of Africa except the Rift Valley in the east and the Maghreb in the north, and much of Australia.

Surprises do occur, for earthquakes may take place other than on the margins of these shields. One occurred at Meckering in Western Australia in 1968, and there have been other examples from time to time. Why an era of earthquake peace in these almost nonseismic areas should be so suddenly and noisily interrupted is not known, although scientists suspect that the underlying crust may have been weakened by previous volcanic activity, and when pent up stresses can no longer be restrained an earthquake will result.

Surprises also occur elsewhere. Although no one could call California a "stable" era, the Long Beach earthquake of 1933 took place on the Newport–Inglewood fault which had only been discovered thirteen years before. The earthquake at San Fernando in 1971 revealed a network of faults underlying the Los Angeles metropolitan area, some of which were quite new.

Western Europe might be considered almost a stable zone by comparison with the hectic earthquake history of the Andes or elsewhere on the Ring of Fire, but in history the region has been shaken from time to time by devastating shocks. A writer attempting to explain an earthquake which struck London and southern England in the year 1580, pointed out that other nations had been smitten with far more regularity, after all in the year A.D. 17, "twelve ancient cities in Asia were overthrown and some also swallowed up into the earth," while Campania and Naples in Italy were "sore affrighted, and molested in A.D. 63," and the "Citie of Basile in Germany was mightelie shaken, and Castles and fortresses to the number almost of an hundred, were upon the shoare of the Rhine utterly overthrown and the hugie Alpes trembled with the like."

While one in 1376 caused extensive damage in Hungary, Carinthia in southern Austria and as far west as Bavaria, "it was thought," added a chronicler, "that the stinking exhalations that this earthquake produced were the cause of that plague which spread over the whole world, which lasted for three years, and which according to calculations, killed a third of the human race."

The Ring of Fire itself girdles the Pacific Ocean in one continuous, although narrow belt. Through much of its journey it is associated with mighty trenches which plunge to great depths and create what are termed island arcs. It is here, on the plate boundaries where an oceanic plate is thrusting vigorously under a continental one that the area of greatest seismicity is located. Volcanic regions of the earth and earthquake regions coincide, although the ring of volcanoes is far less complete and possesses huge gaps – such as that north of the complex of volcanoes around Mexico City, along the greater part of Peru, across the Himalayas and in many other parts of the world.

Passing north from New Zealand lie the islands of Tonga, Samoa, Fiji, the Loyalty Islands, the New Hebrides and the Solomons, all associated with great deeps. There is one deep off the Solomons 3,300 fathoms (5,940 m); one 3,850 fathoms (6,930 m) off the New Hebrides; while off Tonga a huge trough plunges downward to a massive depth of 5,811 fathoms – 34,866 feet (10,459 m) – in comparison Mount Everest is a puny 28,028 feet (8,409 m) high.

Stretching northward, the Ring turns west to embrace the islands of New Britain and New Guinea, and the Moluccas. North of the Moluccas lie the Marianas, a string of islands characterized by a massive trench in places over 5,000 fathoms (9,000 m) deep – and in one, the aptly named Challenger

Deep, the bottom is an incredible 5,938 fathoms (10,688 m) down. Running parallel is an inner arc which encompasses the Philippines where a fault zone runs through the islands from Luzon to Mindanao, and the Bonin Islands, with trenches reaching down to over 4,000 fathoms (7,200 m). The principal arm of the Ring of Fire continues northward to the Japanese archipelago and the seismic arc across the top of the Pacific Ocean composed of the Kurils and the Aleutians, and culminates in the seismic zone of Alaska. This is an area characterized by massive earthquakes; Yakutat in Alaska was shaken by one believed to be of the order of 8.6 magnitude in 1899. In 1903 it was the turn of the Aleutians (8.3 magnitude). The next year, two quakes of 8.3 and 8.1 shook the Russian peninsula of Kamchatka. The Aleutians were hit again in 1906 and in 1915. In 1917 there was another earthquake in Kamchatka. Since then there have been a dozen major earthquakes in the general area of a magnitude of 8.0 or over.

To many people, Japan and earthquakes are almost synonymous and certainly the detailed records of Japanese earthquakes, some of devastating size, reach back to well before the birth of Christ. When John Milne arrived in Tokyo in 1875 it was to find records of over two thousand earthquakes in

To many, Japan is almost considered the "home" of earthquakes, and earthquake records go back for over one thousand years. This vivid and detailed drawing of 1856 depicts the sorry aftermath of an earthquake.

the Japanese archives. More recently, the Mino–Owari quake of 1891, which made the Neo fault across the island of Honshu move by distances as great as twenty-three feet (6.9 m) along a thirty mile (48.3 km) length, can be classified as a major quake. The Kanto quake of 1923 was of 8.3 magnitude, a monster. Since then there have been eight major quakes registering 7.0 magnitude or over on the Richter scale, the largest in 1952. This was a quake of 8.6 on the island of Hokkaido, an area associated with the Kurils/Kamchatka/Aleutian arc across the top of the Pacific.

The recent earthquake (7.5 magnitude) in June 1978, like so many that have struck Japan, was situated off the eastern coast along the great island arc which constitutes the Japanese archipelago. This one had its epicenter sixty miles (96.6 km) from land and the northern part of Honshu, in particular the prefecture of Miyogi, took the brunt. Here 21 people were reported killed, and a further 350 were injured. In Senda, water mains were ruptured, and electricity supplies cut. 180 miles (289.8 km) to the south office workers in Tokyo rushed on to the streets as highrise buildings swayed in a terrifying fashion for a full minute. Apart from a few water pipes bursting, and a few windows crashing on the sidewalk below, there was no substantial damage however.

Private collection

*Japan* After the great earthquake of 1964 at Niigata in northeast Honshu. The piers supporting the bridge have moved and precipitated the roadway into the river.
NOAA/EDS

The great ocean trench system continues off Central and South America – that off Acapulco goes down to a depth of 2,900 fathoms (5,220 m). Off Guatemala the Middle American Trench reaches a depth of 3,600 fathoms (6,480 m), while further south off Chile depths of 4,000 fathoms (7,200 m) have been recorded.

Central America has recently seen two catastrophic quakes, the Managua earthquake in Nicaragua in 1972, and the Guatemala quake in 1976.

There is nothing new about earthquakes in Guatemala. In 1773 this moving account was written: "At the first impact all the buildings fell to the ground. A ship in the middle of the ocean is not moved, not even in the harshest storm, as we saw our pitiful land tremble . . . we rode on a sea of mountains and jungles, sinking in rubble and drowning in the foam of wood and rock. The earth was boiling under our feet as if tired of bearing us . . . making bells ring, the towers, spires, temples, palaces, houses, and even the humblest huts fall; it would not forgive either one for being high or the other for being low." Recently, local seismologists noticed a significant decrease in the number of minor tremors that shook Guatemala each year – five hundred a year in the 1950s to less than half that in the 1960s. But in 1976 an earthquake (7.5 magnitude) struck Guatemala City without warning. 25,000 people were killed, and 77,000 were injured. One million people were left homeless. Damage apart from the loss of life was estimated at $2 billion.

Chile and Peru, and, to a lesser extent, Colombia and Ecuador, have all been shaken by massive quakes since time immemorial. Lima, Peru, was all but destroyed in 1657 by an earthquake which prompted a Peruvian to write of Spain, the occupying power, that even if "not a Mark of the Wrath of Heaven on the Spaniards, [this is] at least a Sign that the Earth is weary

*Peru* Only the massive statue of Christ, and four small trees, remained standing in Yungay after the catastrophic earthquake in 1970.

US Geological Survey

*Central America* The earthquake of 1972 in Managua, Nicaragua, was responsible for the almost total destruction of this street in the town of Taquezal.

EERI Managua Conference Proceedings

of them." 1682 saw another great earthquake in Lima, followed five years later by another. Chile was shaken in 1730 and 1751 by enormous quakes, which seemed to be distant disturbances to the people of Europe, until the great Lisbon disaster four years later brought home to them the fact that they themselves were not immune from this handiwork of the Almighty. In this century, nearly two dozen quakes of 7.5 magnitude or over have taken place in Central and South America.

The whole western seaboard of South America is one of intense, indeed hectic, seismic activity, and has been so since recorded history. It used to be said of Caracas in Venezuela that the people there were as used to earthquakes as those in Mexico to revolutions and certainly the incidences of earth tremors are very high. The Venezuelans characterize several degrees; least of all is the *temblor*, next the *vibracion*, which enlarges to the *tremor* proper. Then comes the *golpe*, which is the kind of shake which can cause broken windows. Further up the scale is the ominous sounding *rasgada*, and worst of all the full-blown *terremoto*. They are so used to earthquakes that there is jokingly said to be a sort of seismic highway running beneath the countryside and quakes appear to stick to well defined tracks along the freeway.

*The Caribbean* 1692 saw the end of the "sin city" and pirate haunt of Port Royal, Jamaica, which collapsed into the sea causing great loss of life. British Library

The Caribbean is another seismic area, and here, for the most part, earthquakes are associated with the edges of the Caribbean plate. The American plate is gradually moving westward and being carried beneath its Caribbean neighbor, building up tremendous forces along the way and driving pieces of the earth's crust and accumulated water down into the interior. Volcanologists believe that this pressure will ultimately be relieved in the form of a gigantic volcanic explosion like the one which occurred at Mont Pelée in Martinique in 1902.

The great quake of 1692 which wiped out the city of Port Royal, and submerged most of it is often cited. But there have been many other quakes in the area. The earthquake of 1907 in Jamaica caused widespread damage and locally reached a very high intensity. Many people rushed into the streets at the first tremor only to find themselves thrown violently to the ground.

To the west of the Ring of Fire, where the Mediterranean–Himalayan or Alpide Belt crosses the subcontinent of India and reaches through Asia Minor to the Mediterranean countries is another seismically active belt.

Aerial photographs have supported the theory that the Indian subcontinent is thrusting under the Asian land mass to create the Himalayas. It has been calculated that India is moving north at a rate of two inches (5 cm) a year. At the eastern end of the Himalayan range lies perhaps the most seismically active part of the world. Here an immense seismic belt some 2,500 miles (4,025 km) long stretches across Tibet and much of China. This is associated with the colossal Tangshan earthquake in northwest China in 1976. For centuries this area of the globe has been shaken by catastrophic earthquakes. One of the most violent was what became known as the Assam earthquake, which was felt in Calcutta, 550 miles (886 km) away from the epicenter and shook an area half the size of Europe.

The whole area is inherently unstable. Since the turn of the century, more than a dozen quakes of 8.0 magnitude or over have been recorded. The Kansu earthquake in 1920 was believed responsible for the deaths of 200,000 people and the whole landscape in an area 280 miles (451 km) by 95 miles (153 km) (equivalent to the whole of New York state east of Syracuse) was totally altered and ten great cities were devastated. Many of the dead were cave dwellers who were entombed for ever, including the four hundred followers of a Mohammedan prophet called Ma the Charitable who had met in conclave to declare a Holy War. A missionary Madame Labrouste, was a horrified witness. "The noise made me suspect an earthquake, so I blew out my lamp and rushed out of doors," she later wrote, "but I was scarcely outside when it was as if someone gave me a great push from behind . . . I kept my legs wide apart like a drunkard, so as not to fall, and I felt a strong turning movement: all those few statues that did not fall from their places were next day found with their faces to the wall. . . . This first and strongest of the shocks lasted two minutes and it was so quickly followed by five or six others that it

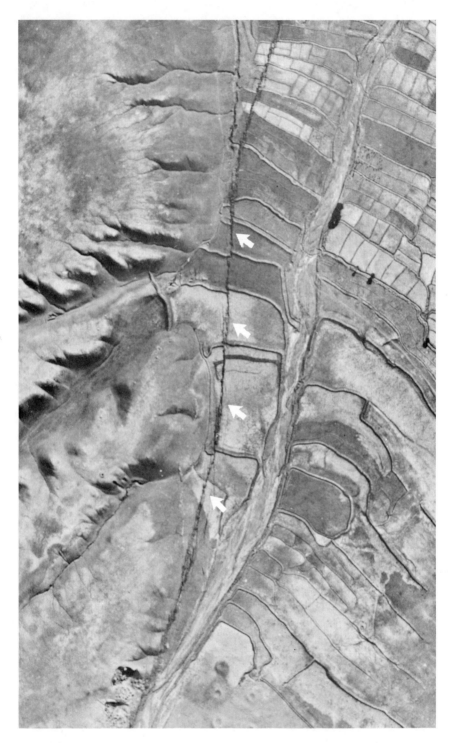

*Iran* Much of the Middle East is a very active seismic area. The fault break shown in this aerial photograph took place in 1968 and resulted in a displacement of ridges and fences of an average of twelve feet (4.2 m).

Professor N.N. Ambraseys

was almost impossible to distinguish between them. . . . The appalling noise of falling houses, the shrieks of men and the bellowing of animals under the ruins were a terrible, terrible sound." This area has the dubious notoriety of having seen the worst earthquake ever known. This was in 1556 when it was estimated that 830,000 people lost their lives.

Passing westward, the Hindu Kush range in north Afghanistan has been the seat of many earthquakes, many of intermediate depth (100–150 miles – 161–242 km – deep) and some of massive size – there have already been three of 8.0 magnitude or over and many lesser ones this century in the Hindu Kush itself or in the nearby Russian Republic of Tadzhikstan.

In this notoriously active seismic belt two thousand quakes are registered annually – in 1977 there were no less than six thousand. The main Russian earthquake research activity is centered here, an effort which started in 1949 after an earthquake which killed some ten thousand people and did immense damage in the Republic of Tadzhikistan.

From the Hindu Kush, the Persian arc spreads in a wide sweep through the Pamir mountains and the Caucasus to Turkey. The area at the eastern end of the Mediterranean is one of peculiar complexity. Here the Arabian Plate, on which stands the Arabian peninsula and Iran, is moving gradually northward, usurping the Turkish Plate, including part of Turkestan. This movement is in turn unseating the Aegean Plate on which rests the Aegean Sea, the Dodecanese Islands and the eastern part of Greece itself. A contrary movement is taking place at the same time, as the North African Plate inches northward into the Eurasian Plate which comprises much of Europe. It was this latter movement, which aeons ago had previously created the Alps, which was responsible for the shattering succession of earthquakes ravaging the Italian Udine region at the head of the Adriatic, around Friuli in May 1976, whose tremors were felt as far away as France and Bulgaria.

The whole of the Near East is inherently unstable and references to earthquakes in the Bible are legion. "The mountains skipped like lambs and the hills like young sheep," wrote one scribe (Psalm 114). A great earthquake in the days of Uzziah, King of Judah, who reigned from 811 to 759 B.C., "shook the ground and rent the Temple" (Kings XIX, verses 11 and 12). In 1566 B.C., so it is reckoned, the walls of Jericho were overthrown by an earthquake. Earlier the passage of the Red Sea was accomplished by the providential upheaval of the ground, and there seems strong evidence that some sort of earth tremor occurred at the Crucifixion (Matthew XXVII, verses 51–3).

Constantinople has been frequently smitten by earthquakes, "wonderfully shaken an whole yeere" described one chronicler, barely disguising his glee at the scourging of so heathen a place. In 1348 another "indured six weeks and reached in the extent of it as far as Hungary and Italy. Twenty-six cities were overthrown by it; Mountains were torn up by the Roots, and several Men, Women and Beasts by that strong Exhalation were turned into Statues of Salt." This must have been a very remarkable earthquake as it was said to have caused the sun to appear as blood "for six hours together," in England, while in Germany the ground was covered with ... grasshoppers.

Elsewhere in the area, Antioch was destroyed many times and often with staggering loss of life. In A.D. 528 during the reign of the Roman Emperor Trajan, a scribe vividly recalled, "There were frightful Lightnings which made the Night as Light as Day, preceeded with dreadful Thunderbolts that threw down stately buildings, killed many men . . . the Sea wrought, the waves swelled, the Earth was shaken, and Darkness was raised that People could not see nor hear one another, nor scarcely breathe. Trees were pluckt up by the Roots, and multitudes buried in the Ruines of their own Houses." It was said that the earth had opened and devoured the city. In this quake it was estimated that thirty thousand people lost their lives, and Trajan only escaped by jumping through a window. Sixty years later, in the reign of Saint Gregory the Great, a massive death toll of sixty thousand was caused by yet another major earthquake, yet the place was rebuilt again. Further south, the city of Baalbek was destroyed three times between 1664 and 1759, but it was to survive for many years after.

The Aegean area has been subjected to massive earthquakes since the time of earliest recorded history – and doubtless long before that. In remote antiquity, twelve thousand years before, according to Plato, Atlantis was swallowed up. Between 3000 and 2500 B.C. the whole of the known world was shaken by tremendous upheavals. In 1900 B.C. a violent earthquake ruined most of the towns and cities in Attica, and this was followed by a devastating tsunami, the whole terrible event being known as the Ogygrian deluge. Four hundred years later what became known as the Deucalion flood wiped out Thessaly. Nearer the present, in 476 B.C., armies marching on Boeotia were severely shaken by an earthquake, and taking this as a sign of disapproval by the gods, they prudently turned back. Almost one hundred years later, in 373 B.C. a strip of land along the Gulf of Corinth several miles long and over a mile (1.6 km) wide sank beneath the waters. More recently, in 1947, a 7.0 magnitude earthquake took place in the Peloponnese. In 1948 an earthquake hit Karpathos; another occurred in the same year on the island of Levkas; in 1953 no less than five quakes shook the mainland of Greece; and in 1978 a major quake struck Salonika.

Further north, Yugoslavia is no stranger to earthquakes. The Skopje quake in 1963, 6.0 magnitude, caused widespread damage and great loss of life.

Italy, particularly southern Italy, Calabria and Sicily, has been devastated

*Yugoslavia* International relief after the disastrous earthquake at Skopje in July 1963 reached an unprecedented level. By the end seventy-two nations had participated in rescue, rehabilitation or rebuilding in the capital of Macedonia.

Skopje

by earthquakes on many occasions. In 1622 several eye-witnesses reported the shape of an elephant in the sky, while armies were heard fighting in the air, waters in many places ran like blood and "impetuous Tempests" overthrew many towers. Five years later a great earthquake struck the town of Apulia in southern Italy and occasioned a miraculous escape as a bell fell from a church tower directly on top of a little girl standing beneath – and completely enclosed her doing no harm.

Other parts of Italy are by no means immune. It was the turn of Umbria and then of Tuscany in 1948. The previous year Breschia was damaged, and in 1948 a quake north of Lake Garda was felt as far away as Switzerland. More recently has occurred the tragic series of quakes in Friuli in North Italy.

It was nearing the close of a typical, warm early summer's day – May 6, 1976, when the quake struck. At 8:55 P.M. a short, sharp shock rattled a few window panes and caused the dishes to clink on the shelves. At 9:00 P.M.

*Sicily* Messina in Sicily is not only subject to the waywardness of the volcano Etna. It has also been subject to many massive earthquakes such as this one of 1783 which is believed to have killed thirty thousand people.

British Museum

precisely another, stronger shock caused a number of people to leave their homes in concern. Then, two minutes later, a colossal tremor shook an area of North Italy covering forty square miles (103.6 sq. km) in the Friuli Autonymous District around the ancient town of Udine.

Survivors of that terrible evening vividly remember what they witnessed. Drivers recall that their cars lost control and skidded across the roads as though on ice. Some looking to the north and the mountains, remember a strange glow illuminating the distant hills, which silhouetted against the sky, were jerking up and down like an animated cartoon. Others remember the appalling crash of disintegrating houses and falling masonry, for the damage throughout the region was tremendous.

Out of 119 communities in the region, 41 were totally destroyed and 45 severely damaged. The towns of Tarcento and Gemona were completely demolished, every building wrecked or so badly damaged that it had to be abandoned and the townships evacuated. Three-quarters of the houses in the area had been built many years before with walls of coarse masonry bonded insecurely with thick joints of lime or clay mortar and plastered over. Most of these gave way as the walls caved outward, and the heavy floors, ceilings and roofs crashed down on the unfortunate inmates. Other houses, some with their walls weakened where pipes and drains had been inserted, suffered the same fate.

The narrow streets of the little towns and villages proved a death trap. As

*North Italy* North Italy is less prone to earthquakes than southern parts of the Italian peninsula. Sicily and the town of Udine in the Friuli Autonymous province had been mercifully free of earthquakes for many decades until the succession of shocks in May 1976 when nearly two thousand people lost their lives.

The Times

the terrified inhabitants rushed out they were caught by falling masonry and balconies and buried, many crushed to death under a mountain of fallen debris. In all, 965 people lost their lives, and a further 2,000 were injured, as a result of this 6.5 earthquake, the most severe known in that area of Italy where the Alpide fault runs diagonally across the northern part of the country. Seventy thousand people were forced to live in tents, and come the winter, there were still forty thousand under temporary shelter.

Four months after the series of quakes, when the inhabitants were busy repairing the damage, a further two earthquakes shattered the Friuli region again. The courage that had sustained them throughout their long ordeal collapsed, as did many of the half-repaired houses. It was too much. With nerves on edge, and in a mental condition where the banging of a door, or the passing of a noisy motorcycle could cause panic, people began to leave. "We have nothing left," a sorrowful man was heard to say, "except our eyes to cry with."

In Rumania, northeast of Friuli, an earthquake of 7.2 on the Richter scale, considerably greater than the Italian quake, struck Transylvania ten months later, eighty miles (129 km) north of the capital Bucharest.

*Rumania* The tragic earthquake in March 1977 in Rumania's capital, Bucharest, caused over two thousand deaths, and the unpleasant discovery that some modern buildings were far from earthquake-proof. This was a *four*-story apartment block before the quake.　　　Professor N.N Ambraseys

A colossal quake, the worst since 1922, it had its focus sixty miles (96.6 km) beneath the Carpathian Mountains which cushioned some of the force. Nevertheless, the damage in Bucharest was widespread. Casualties in the city were believed to total 1,800; 32 apartment blocks were completely destroyed; a further 160 were damaged. Within miles of the epicenter, at Ploesti, Eastern Europe's largest oil-producing complex, three hundred wells were damaged. One hundred and fifty miles (242 km) to the south there was colossal industrial damage to factories and plant. The quake made buildings shudder and walls crack as far away as Belgrade and Sofia. The shock was even felt in Moscow 850 miles (1,369 km) off. But the damage of this earthquake, the first major quake to strike a European city in modern times was devastating. It was estimated to have put back the Rumanian economy by ten years.

Across the Mediterranean in the Maghreb and the Atlas Mountains, towns and cities have often been shaken, sometimes with devastating results. Algiers was partially destroyed in 1716. In 1755 the Lisbon earthquake also caused damage to the whole northwestern African coast and the toll of deaths was as high as at Lisbon itself. In 1954 Orléansville was badly damaged; in 1960 the tragic quake at Agadir caused the death of over twelve thousand.

*Morocco* In ten seconds the town of Agadir in Morocco was all but obliterated in the earthquake of 1960 and twelve thousand people were killed. The ground was found to have moved by as much as four feet (1.22 m) horizontally and four feet vertically, and modern buildings proved as vulnerable as the old.

NOAA/EDS

*France* Other parts of Europe have also experienced earthquakes from time to time. Revelers enjoying the Mardi Gras in Nice on the Côte d'Azur in 1887 found their pleasures rudely interrupted.

Illustrated London News

The Pyrenees between France and Spain are no stranger to earthquakes. One in 1660 killed many hundreds of people and wrecked many houses, but the earthquake was looked upon as a miracle. For a massive ground movement had shifted a church which had been the subject of a dispute over ownership between the French and the Spaniards. Now it stood intact no less than half a league on the French side of the border.

There have been a number of earthquakes in Britain. The biggest occurred in 1931 with its epicenter in the North Sea, but there is, broadly speaking, a general stability in Great Britain, although certain areas are more seismically active than others. The great Glen Fault in the Highlands of Scotland, which stretches from Inverness in the north via Oban to the Isle of Mull is one such site. Another is along the Highland Border Fault which reaches across Scotland from Stonehaven south of Aberdeen, through the town of Stirling on the River Forth, to Rothesay west of Glasgow. Here Comrie in the Trossachs, and Menstrie at the foot of the Ochil Hills, are most frequently shaken.

Elsewhere and from time to time, different areas have been shaken – as recorded in various annals of differing authenticity and reliability – but on the whole, these have been comparatively mild affairs. Thus, in 1134, when King Henry I was about to set sail for Normandy, according to one chronicle, "flames of fire burst forth with great violence out of certain rifts of the earth." In 1185, all England, and especially the cathedral city of Lincoln was shaken by an earthquake, during which the cathedral and many other buildings were damaged. This was described as "a sore earthquake . . . such a one as the like had not been heard of in England since the beginning of the world." Sixty years later the country was shaken by a series of earthquakes. Kent was smitten in 1246, and it was London's turn the following year; that of Somerset and parts of Wales two years after that, when the cathedrals of Wells and Saint David's were damaged by an earthquake said to have been felt as far afield as North Italy and beyond. London again suffered in 1250 when a quake of a rather minor nature caused few casualties but threw down the Stone Gate and Bulwark on the Tower of London recently built by King Henry III – it was rebuilt but suffered the same fate from another tremor before the century was out.

In 1580, a major quake struck the southern half of England, and the tremors and damage spread to much of Holland and parts of Germany and France as well. This was a date immortalized in Shakespeare's *Romeo and Juliet* "'tis since the earthquake now eleven years," one of the characters in the play declares. This was clearly an event remembered at the time for the great clock bell in the Palace of Westminster "strake of itselfe against ye hammer with shaking, as divers clockes and bells in the City and elsewhere did ye like," – such as at York where they "Struck the very Stones out of the Buildings."

It was all beyond understanding. Some wondered if this expression of

God's will was due to the unparalleled "Looseness and untimely Liberty" exhibited by "Youth" and the like "Unsteadiness and want of Discretion" in "Age." Condemned too was the fact that "Men have taken up the garish Attire and nice Behaviour of Women; and Women, transformed from the Kind have gotten the Apparel of Men," while "Honest and modest Shame-facedness, the preserver of all Virtues, is so highly disliked that it is thought of some Folks, scarce tolerable in Children. . . ."

*Great Britain* England has rarely been troubled by earthquakes, but one in 1884 near Colchester in Essex caused a good deal of damage and a lot of consternation.

1692, as well as being the year Port Royal was destroyed, was the year of what came to be called the Great East Anglian Earthquake, which also shook parts of the Continent, although it was most severe in the eastern counties of England. In Colchester in the county of Essex, some masons were repairing the tower of a church when they had the unnerving experience of seeing the steeple split "so wide that they could have put their hand into the crack or cleft," which, however, immediately shut up again. Elsewhere in the country, chimneys collapsed, "divers old buildings and peeces of churches" fell to the ground and ladies were "affrighted" when tables started to move and rattle. Later a number of people complained of a giddiness in the head.

The world's oceans are no strangers to earthquakes. In the center of the Atlantic lies another seismically active area. Here the mid-ocean ridges witness frequent earthquakes. A similar ridge down the eastern side of the Pacific is another area of intense seismological activity.

The mid-Atlantic ridge starts east of Greenland, includes Iceland, and runs down the center of the ocean sending off a side-shoot which encompasses the Azores and links with the Alpide belt. From there it passes down between the continents of South America and Africa until it takes a sharp eastward bend and approaches India from the south. A smaller Pacific mid-ocean belt swings westward from Chile and then northward, in a great loop to rejoin the continent in Central America, taking in the Galapagos Islands on its way.

Smaller belts exist elsewhere. The East African belt runs northward up the famous Rift Valley to link with the Red Sea and then, via the Gulf of Aqaba and the Dead Sea to merge in the greater Alpide belt as well. If the

The Charleston earthquake of 1886.     quake.
Camping out in City Park after the                    USGS (J.K. Hillers)

Ring of Fire accounts for the larger part of the world's earthquakes each year, the mid-ocean and the East African belts provide most of the remainder.

In the United States, by far the greater proportion of earthquakes occur along and west of the Rockies, with a number of quakes in the mountains themselves, and some reaching down into New Mexico, Nevada and Utah.

The Mississippi Valley is another earthquake-prone area, while scattered quakes have taken place from time to time in the eastern states; of these, the earthquake which hit Charleston, South Carolina, in 1886 is the best known.

Without warning, the quake hit at nine o'clock on the night of August 31. There was a faint tremor at first which was succeeded by a tremendous roar as the quake struck. Furniture, and other movable objects vibrated violently, and the shock was so complex that many pictures ended up facing the wall. The older houses stood up well, but there were few which did not suffer some damage, and the college buildings in Charleston were so battered that they eventually had to be pulled down.

There were about a hundred casualties, and many more than that were injured. What witnesses best remembered was the almost total eerie quietness between shocks; it was as though the world was holding its breath waiting to see what was to happen next. The night was very dark, and further

Charleston 1886. Wreckage in one of the streets. Wooden houses stood up much better than apparently more solidly built buildings.   USGS

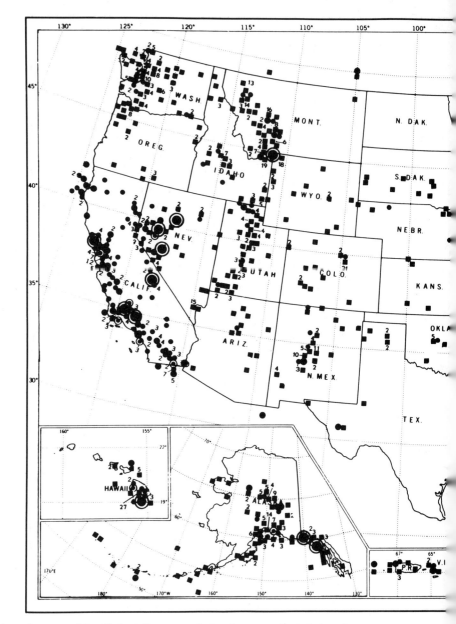

Earthquake map of the United States, showing major earthquakes up to 1970, including those in Alaska.

It has been concluded that those areas most at risk now are San Francisco; Los Angeles; Salt Lake City –

shocks at two o'clock and four o'clock in the morning kept everybody apprehensive and nervous.

Ground movement was considerable. Earth waves were reported by a number of witnesses. Jets of water, mud and sand were seen across a wide area, and there were many fissures, giving off sulfuric fumes although these were rarely more than an inch or two (2.5–5 cm) across. Twisted railroad

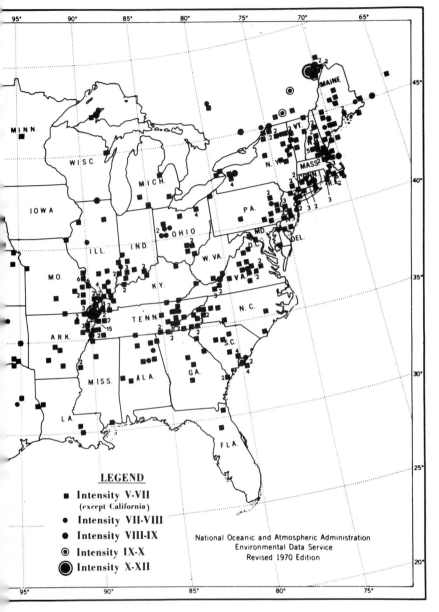

LEGEND

■ Intensity V-VII
  (except California)
● Intensity VII-VIII
● Intensity VIII-IX
◉ Intensity IX-X
◉ Intensity X-XII

National Oceanic and Atmospheric Administration
Environmental Data Service
Revised 1970 Edition

Ogden; Puget Sound; Hawaii;          Charleston, South Carolina.
St Louis – Memphis; Anchorage;
Fairbanks; Boston; Buffalo; and

NEIS

tracks were evidence enough of how very violent the earth movement had been in some places.

The quake was strong enough to cause minor panic in several cities. Chandeliers were set swinging in New York City, one reporter there noticed that "desks seemed to be on rockers and move like cradles," another said that he had been thrown from his chair. In Vicksburg, a council meeting was hurriedly adjourned as many councillors became "sea-sick" on account of the oscillations. In Chicago, windows rattled in their frames, and people walking on the streets felt dizzy and complained of vertigo. In Cincinnati, compositors on a newspaper were so alarmed that they jumped from windows on to some low roofs below their offices in their fright.

It has been estimated that there were two epicentral regions about fourteen miles (22.5 km) apart, but the quake was felt over a vast area. The main shock took place at 9:51 P.M. at Charleston, and this reached Jacksonville, Florida (300 miles – 483 km – away) Baltimore and New York City (respectively 500 miles – 805 km and 700 miles – 1,127 km away) three minutes later, at 9:54 P.M. A minute and a half after that, New Haven, Connecticut felt it and there was a faint tremor in Boston. But the sensation was noticed as far afield as Michigan and Ontario to the north, the Gulf of Mexico and even Bermuda, 1,000 miles (1,610 km) away, to the south.

This earthquake is still looked on with some surprise by seismologists, for the eastern states are not considered to be a very active earthquake zone and a quake of this magnitude is mercifully rare. Yet each year nearly two dozen quakes occur of sufficient size to be felt by those near them, and literally thousands of fault lines crisscross the geological map – although these are mainly very deep.

The confidence, almost amounting to complacency in some quarters, that these districts are almost earthquake-free, has caused a growing disquiet in seismological circles. For, in the densely populated areas of this part of the United States, an earthquake of even moderate magnitude is likely to cause damage and loss of life which together would amount to a major disaster. One on the Charleston scale, in say the northeast where there are many nuclear plants could cause an immense disaster. As a result, a good deal of money has recently been made available to increase seismological monitoring of the area.

But it is to the western states, and to California in particular, that all minds turn when mention is made of an earthquake in the United States. 90 percent of American earthquakes take place in California and Western Nevada, and most are associated with the San Andreas fault zone – parts of which have been distressingly active over the past two hundred years – and the faults which separate the Sierra Nevada from the Great Basin. Earthquakes in this area of the United States are shallow and clearly associated with fault movement, and quakes in the past have been responsible for some quite dramatic fault adjustments. No less than eight sizable quakes have occurred in the last one hundred and fifty years which have caused actual surface rupture. Perhaps the greatest of these was what became known as the Owens Valley Earthquake of 1872, of a magnitude believed to have been in excess of 8.3 on the Richter scale, and which holds the dubious distinction of being the greatest earthquake in American history, south of the Canadian border.

The quake struck at two-thirty on the morning of Good Friday, March 26,

1872. There was no warning, only a sudden first shock which hit the area like a thunderbolt. Opinions differ as to its duration. Some said it lasted for half a minute; others that it was three times as long; but it was felt across much of western America, all along the Sierras. The greatest damage was reserved for the western slopes of the Sierra Nevada, fortunately a region then sparsely populated. Nevertheless, the little township of Lone Pine was all but demolished and of the tiny population of 250, 27 were killed and a further 56 injured (this from an overall death toll of 60.)

A witness described the onset of the quake as sounding like the firing of a "whole park of artillery, with the rattle of musketry between." When the tremor passed, it was succeeded by the barking and howling of dogs, the rumble of falling masonry and the creaking of timbers in those few houses that did not succumb. Most of the houses were constructed of flimsy adobe, and nearly all collapsed immediately crushing the occupants. Second and third shocks after dawn, and lesser aftershocks which continued for three months, destroyed most of the remainder.

The effects of this quake were considerable, and ground sinking was reported in a number of places. Along some rivers fish were cast onto the banks. Fissures – great parallel fractures in the ground – were reported by many observers. Faulting reached no less than twenty-three feet (6.9 m) vertically and nearly as much laterally, while a fierce wave slopped the water in Owens Lake. There were several authenticated reports of mysterious lights, and some said that they had seen fires in the mountains, which went on for nearly half an hour; others reported streams of fire as the sides of canyons and hills collapsed into the rivers and valleys below. At Camp Cody, two hundred miles (322 km) from Lone Pine, a string of military mules pulling Army wagons were thrown off their feet by the violence of the shock. A tidal wave occurred on the coast of California. It was even said that Mexico City, 1,700 miles (2,737 km) away, felt the tremor – but that is considered an improbable report.

Scientists believe that a major Californian earthquake is imminent, not in the Sierra Nevada, but somewhere along the six hundred mile (966 km) San Andreas fault which stretches in a huge fracture believed to be twenty miles (32.2 km) deep in places from northern California into Mexico, and which denotes the division between the North Pacific and the great American Plates. In places the San Andreas is clear cut, but in others it breaks into myriad lesser faults. This is particularly so in the San Francisco area and south of the city where the Hayward and Calveras Faults run roughly parallel; between Santa Barbara and Los Angeles where a mass of lesser faults mark the map like the veining in marble; and south of Los Angeles itself where the San Andreas fault breaks into a number of parallel faults running roughly northeast-southwest and which stretch toward Lower California. Of these, the best known are the Newport-Inglewood fault running from Los Angeles to San Diego, and the San Jacinto leading toward the Imperial fault running from San Bernardino southward.

But it is on the areas between these quakes that seismological eyes are turned, and not without a good deal of apprehension. Here are a number of interesting, and disturbing phenomena. It was in the late 1960s and early 1970s that it was noticed that a huge area – 23,400 square miles (60,000 sq km) – north of Los Angeles and astride the San Andreas fault appeared to have risen by as much as 8 inches (20 cm). It is still rising. This is the notorious

The San Andreas fault. Like a great surgical scar across the landscape, the San Andreas fault carves its way across California east of San Diego.

A map of the San Andreas fault complex showing how it criss-crosses the densely populated Los Angeles area. Place names with dates indicate earthquakes.

USGS

Palmdale Bulge, astride the San Andreas Fault, southeast of the location of the Fort Tejon quake of 1857 – an earthquake considered to have been in order of 8.0 magnitude and which shifted over 186 miles (300 km) of fault by as much as thirty feet (9 m) in some places. No one knows what the Palmdale Bulge presages, or what it will do. It is possible, some think, that it might deflate, but most seismologists believe that this is unlikely. Nevertheless, it does indicate a disturbing restlessness on the San Andreas fault itself.

A similar dome to the Palmdale Bulge was observed before the San Fernando quake of 1971, but this was not then associated with the quake itself. It had been hoped that this earthquake which was of magnitude 6.6 and was felt in Mexico, the states of Arizona and Nevada and as far north as Yosemite

Earthquakes in the United States are by no means exclusive to the western side of the Rockies. This is the amazing result of one at Kosmo, Utah, on the northern edge of the Great Salt Lake, in 1934.

NOAA/EDS

National Park, had released all the pent up energy latent in the San Andreas fault system, at least in the immediate area, but now seismologists are not so sure and fear that this was not after all the long awaited "Big One." That this will strike someday, is the almost unanimous opinion of experts, but whether it will be before the century is out, or before the decade is out, or somewhere in between is less clear. But when it does, the chilling surmise is that it will strike at the densely populated areas of either San Francisco, or Los Angeles. The highest probability is that there will be a repetition of the 1857 quake sixty miles (96.6 km) northwest of Los Angeles, or a repeat of the

1906 San Francisco disaster – neither option is particularly comforting.

The periodicity or frequency of earthquakes is the measure of the seismicity of an area. This is of interest not only for purely scientific reasons, or to help "prospect" a region seismologically, but for more immediately practical purposes, to help engineers or those constructing buildings. There have been few large quakes in recent years, but many more deaths. This is a direct reflection on the location of towns in relation to geological faults, and the quality of building and construction in earthquake zones. It is vitally important for an engineer to know that within say a space of twenty years X quakes with a local intensity Y are likely to take place and that there is a reasonable probability that his construction will have to withstand such forces. For insurance purposes, the seismicity of a region is of equal importance in assessing earthquake risk.

Such seismicity calculations may give the likelihood of how many earthquakes will take place over a certain period of time, but it will not reveal the whole story. Some areas have "active" periods, some have "quiet" ones. The assessment of when these will take place is closely linked with earthquake prediction, a study which has fascinated man for centuries and which is rapidly beginning to play an active and credible part in the saving of lives.

Yet the pattern behind a sequence of earthquakes is still obscure – this is not to be confused with what are called microseisms, a profusion of baby tremors, which may, or may not lead to a bigger quake. For, as certain areas are more prone to earthquakes than others, it has also been noticeable that at certain times earthquakes have occurred almost in unison. As recently as August 1976, there were strong earthquakes in close succession as far apart as the Philippines, China and Italy. In November of the same year, in the space of just two days, there were quakes in a broad belt from the Pacific Ocean to Greece – in northern Greece, Iran, China, Japan and the Philippines. The pattern here is hard to see, harder still to predict, yet this rash of quakes indicates a certain restlessness in the earth, which, for reasons as yet unknown, comes to a head at these particular times. They demonstrate only too clearly the awesome power in the accumulating strain gathering in the earth beneath our feet.

# 4
# Earthquake Effects

THE HOUSES SEEMED to leap upward, and then returned to their former position. The earth opened up and swallowed forty horsemen, whose cries could be heard long after. The bells in the churches sounded by themselves, and hailstones as big as ostrich eggs rained down on the unhappy people. The moon appeared to be on fire, and blood-red rain soaked the panic-stricken inhabitants. In this way a medieval observer described an earth-quake which struck England in A.D. 1089. He noted that some weeks after the shock little children had the smallpox. To a primitive mind the whole was so utterly beyond their understanding and comprehension that their imagination ran riot; even to more sophisticated minds, earthquake effects verge on the uncanny, the supernatural and the fantastic.

The immediate effects of an earthquake affect different people in different ways, according to an observer of the 1580 London earthquake: "Some doubtless at their prayers, and hearing godly Sermons, whome as men, it must needes amaze, or bring into a muse. Some at the Taverne, and upon their Alebench and therefore might well suspect that it was long of their liquor. Some in earnest conference of worldly affaires, and so per-adventure they tooke small or no regard at all of it. Some in ydlenesse alone, and these of likelyhoode it might sorely abash. Some at game, and therefore not much moved. Some at common Playes, who as I understand, were horribly troubled. Some in wanton talks and disport, whom it might well affright. Some perhappes worse occupied, whome I would counsell to be more carefull of the Lordes suddaine visitation. Some fast asleepe, and therefore senseless: and some walking the streetes and fields, or carried on Horseback, or in Coaches, and therefore not able to discerne of any such matter. Some that were above in their Chambers, judged that some violence had bin done to their houses below, found fault with tumbling and trampling above. Some imputed the ratling of wainescot to rattes and Weesels; the shaking of the beddes, tables and stooles, to Dogges: the quaking of their walles to their neyghbours rushing on tother side."

To most earthquake sufferers it is not the dancing buildings, the corruga-tions of the ground, or the sight of sturdy trees almost touching the ground as they sway from side to side, but the noise which is most terrifying. The noise varies. On the whole it is more generally heard on hard rather than soft ground, and sometimes it is difficult indoors to separate the noise of the earthquake from the secondary noises of groaning masonry, creaking houses and tumbling plaster. But out of doors the low grumbling sound is unmistakable. Sometimes it takes the form of short explosions or a succession of bangs – indeed on one occasion the captain of a ship in a British fleet at anchor in the Black Sea was disturbed by the noise of an earthquake and made hurriedly for shelter, sending his commodore a stiffly worded signal that in future he would be obliged if it were possible to inform him when torpedo practice was to take place!

Earthquake noise is often described as preceding the tremor, but that is because the initial compression wave which accompanies the sound was not strong enough to be felt. In general, though, the sound is of a very low pitch and near the point on the scale of audibility when sound and feeling are almost the same.

Some have likened the noise to that of a carriage or cart passing over cobbles. One called it a hollow, frightful murmur; to another it reminded him of the moaning of the wind or the rumbling of thunder. It was like the clanking of chains to one seafarer; a "hizzing hollow report" was how a citizen of London described it. It vividly recalled to one observer the "clatter which is sometimes heard on board an ocean-going steamer in very rough weather, when a heavy sea strikes the ship and all the crockery laid out for dinner is suddenly thrown to the floor."

The duration of these rumblings is hard to determine. In early times,

In popular imagination earthquakes swallowed humans and animals, although incidents of this actually occurring are rare.

Ground deformation led to this      in Japan in 1891.
remarkable twisting of a railway line

Professor N.N. Ambraseys

when timepieces were carried only by the rich, and ordinary people had little awareness of time, the duration of earthquake noise was difficult to calculate. "Sodenlie," described one, "and in the twingling of an eye the same noyse was as thoughe yt had been round aboute the hearers; and therwith began a most feirce and terrible earthquake, which with the noyse aforesaid and other circumstances contynued not above the tyme as we commonlie call yt of a paternoster while."

Sometimes the precise moment when the rumblings start or finish, or when the maximum point is reached, is obscure. If earthquake noise can continue for a long time, earthquake shaking can continue for hours, days and even sometimes weeks. Under such circumstances, time ceases to have any meaning and the victims become almost concussion-crazy, oblivious to anything but their own safety. It was said that in a Japanese earthquake in A.D. 745, the shaking continued for sixty hours on end. Another earthquake two hundred years later lasted for three hundred days.

Intensities are very local, and may be worse in a moderate quake than in one of a greater magnitude. Within a few miles of the epicenter it may be

Professor Agassiz was ignominiously thrown from the niche in which he was standing at Stanford University in the San Francisco earthquake of 1906.

University of California, Berkeley

difficult to stand upright. In Jamaica during the earthquake of 1907, someone noticed that the "grass lawn was gently undulating, and tipping the wicker chair in which I sat. The pavement was visibly moving and I was quite thrown on my face." In a great earthquake which struck Java in the East Indies in the nineteenth century, a missionary wrote that he was "started by a peculiar shivering as I sat in my chair. At first I imagined I was seized with a terrible feverless ague, but I was soon undeceived by the increasing bumping of my bottles and possessions and the vehement beseeching of *Tuhan Allah* and the loud exclamations of the natives."

The shock can be intense and sharp. In the same Jamaica earthquake, one man was thrown bodily through the panels of a door and when he came to his senses found his head stuck through it; another found himself thrown head first into a barrel. Oxen and other animals were seen to stand sideways to the motion of the ground with legs wide apart. At Port Royal, so violent were the shocks that it was impossible to stand at all, and people were thrown bodily to the ground where they lay with their arms and legs spreadeagled to prevent being tumbled about while the earth heaved and tossed around and beneath them.

The motion itself was described by Sir William Hamilton as being accompanied by a rumbling noise and beginning usually with a horizontal shaking, and ending with the *vorticose* – which is the motion which has ruined most of the buildings in the province, he added. In early earthquake treatises ground movement is graphically described as being either *vorticose, orizontale* or *oscillatorio*.

"The manner of the shaking of euerie Earthquake is of three sortes," said Seneca, the Roman philosopher in an early translation. "For eyther it shaketh towards one side and is lyke a certayne trembling or rocking, & this is a token of a great store of ye exhalation: or else it lyfteth right up in the middest, & letteth fall againe, after the manner of the Pulse . . . or else it seemeth to be compounded of them twaine, and at the same instant dooeth bothe rocke and lyft up the earth together, and with the diversities of motion & Dauncing, as it were, it rattleth, and butteth the houses and buyldings together."

Darwin was present when a mild earthquake struck Valdivia in Chile in 1835. "It came on suddenly," he wrote afterward, "and lasted for two minutes. I had no difficulty in standing upright, but the motion made me almost giddy. It was something like the movement of a vessel in a little cross ripple, or still more like that felt by a person skating over very thin ice, which bends under the weight of his body."

Another described the sensation as being like a dog shaking itself when it comes out of the water, or a horse twitching as a fly alights on its back.

One man observed that the earthquake motion was more evidently "perceived by people standing; most by those that were sitting; least by such as were walking; and in upper storeys of houses more than in lower, or in cellars. Some, coming down stairs, were in danger of being thrown forward; several sitting in chairs, and hearing the hollow thundering noise, and thinking it was a coach passing by, when they attempted to get up, to see what it was, they were thrown back again into their chair, while some heard the wainscot crackle."

A most vivid description emerges from the New England earthquake which John Winthrop experienced. A companion wrote: "The earthquake began with a roaring noise in the north-west like thunder at a distance; and this became fiercer as the earthquake drew nearer. The first sensation was like a pulse, or an undulation, resembling that of a long rolling, swelling sea; and the swell was so great, that a person was obliged to run and catch hold of something, to prevent being thrown down. . . . The bed on which Mr. W.

lay, was now tossed from side to side; the whole house was prodigiously agitated; the beams cracked, as if all would presently be shaken to pieces."

In many places in New England pewter was thrown to the floor; a number of chimneys were leveled; others tilted at alarming angles, still others were twisted as though by some malevolent hand. A few roofs were broken by the tumbling chimneys; gable ends occasionally collapsed. The weather vane on the Faneuiel Hall in Boston fell to the ground, its five inch (12 cm) wooden spindle snapped off clean, while at Springfield eighty miles (129 km) away, their weather vane was badly bent. Otherwise there was little damage, except that a brand new wooden cistern was shattered by the violent agitation of the liquid within it, but across the country stone fences suffered severely.

The effect of an earthquake shock on a ship at sea can be violent but it is seldom disastrous. In the New England quake a ship seventy leagues off Boston was shaken so violently that those on board felt they had run aground, until they discovered there was fifty fathoms of water below them. Those ships in harbor were so agitated that those aboard felt they "were bouncing up and down on the bottom." Many fish, dead and dying, floated to the surface.

The violence of an earthquake in 1816 broke ropes and spars, but this was unusual. A more normal effect was vividly described by people in boats on the River Thames during the London earthquake of 1750 who likened their

The weather vane on Faneuiel Hall in        of November, 1755.
Boston was snapped off in the shock            British Museum

This locomotive was thrown from its tracks in the San Francisco quake of 1906. It was standing in a siding at the time.

experience to the same sensation that would be felt if a porpoise, or some great fish, had heaved and thumped at the bottom of the craft.

The noise and the shaking of solid earth is terrifying, but it is the visible effects which remain most vividly in the memories of earthquake survivors as their whole world, which up to then had been so solid and indestructible and understandable, is subjected to forces which appear beyond reason. Sidewalks seem to dance; roads roll and undulate like waves in the sea; and solid surfaces appear to open up in great fissures and then close again. Stone pillars are seen to twist and ripple.

Sometimes these effects do occur, as is clearly shown by physical evidence, but often these phenomena are nothing more than hallucinations. Subsequent examination shows no break or crack in structures; the fissured sidewalk is as sound as it ever was; pillars are still standing; walls have remained intact. Yet observers, including scientists, have claimed to have actually seen these events. One explanation may be that these hallucinations are due

USGS (G.K. Gilbert)

to disturbance in the inner mechanism of the ear – akin to a very severe attack of sea sickness.

Captain McMurdo was taking an evening walk on the ramparts of the old fort at Poorbunder in what is now Pakistan, when the great Indian Earthquake of 1819 struck – a quake which caused damage as far afield as Katmandu in the north, to Pondicherry in the south, from Calcutta in the east, to the great mountains of Baluchistan in the west. Later he wrote, "I felt a violent shock beneath my feet . . . looking at the same time forwards, I saw the stone parapet at two yards distance violently agitated by a quick, short wave-like motion, bending in and out with the greatest pliability, and with the vibration of about a foot, and attended with an incessant hissing, cracking noise . . . I was obliged to run back towards a ramp and all the time there was a sensation like running along an elevated and elastic plank, the ends of which are supported. . . . It certainly was terrific to behold hills, towers, and houses, the stability of which we had been in the habit of considering as proof against every power, and against the lapse of centuries, rocking to and fro, or rising and sinking, while the former sent forth clouds of dust, and perhaps smoke, and the latter crumbled into rubbish."

Many reports of earthquakes speak of ghostly lights which accompanied the tremors. In olden times these were often attributed to meteors or the ignition of inflammable "vapors." Some may certainly be attributed to the viewers' imagination, some to more modern phenomena such as pylons, or electric cables touching and sparking. But the reports are too frequent, too substantiated to be wholly dismissed out of hand as the imaginings of over-fertile minds.

In an earthquake in 1633 many witnesses reported a globe of fire rising from the earth which then fell into the sea. This was followed by a fierce hailstorm with hailstones as big as "musket balls." Meteors and balls of light are common phenomena associated with earthquakes in history. As recently as the 1975 Liaoning quake in China there were many fully sub-stantiated reports that the whole horizon was lit by some ghostly light at the time of the earthquake. The presence of these lights, or flames, or "prodi-gious fires" is not proved – but nor is it disproved. Certainly peculiar electric effects have been reported on many occasions.

In the Owens Valley earthquake in California, a local printer was astonished to see paper after going through the press appear to float in the air when he passed his hand over it. As many as one hundred sheets at a time seemed to have a will of their own and wanted to adhere to his hand like iron filings to a magnet. A watchmaker in another quake found that he could not place the balance back in a watch he was repairing, the pieces seemed to stick to the needle he was using.

Perhaps the earliest record of such electric activity was during an earth-quake in Italy in 1808, when a Volta's electrometer recorded remarkable disturbances. Since then there have been many reports of strange electrical activity and electric arcing before and during earthquakes. A lot of research is currently going on into electric phenomena, but although a number of theories have been propounded, the unusual light and electrical activity associated with some earthquakes remains a mystery.

Water effects are constantly recurring phenomena before and during earthquakes. Wells rise and fall; fountains stop flowing; others gush yellow or red water, tasting foul and smelling strongly of sulfur.

At Concepcion, Chile, in 1835, the water turned black and smelled of decay. This emission of sulfurous fumes and other odors was so intense that it blackened the white hull of the American ship *Lancaster* anchored at Callao during the Lima earthquake of 1865.

Steam and smoke, water, mud and sand spouts have at times been ejected with such force as to "reach the height of the tallest trees." Sometimes this water has been "boiling" and the sand at the sea's edge hot to the touch,

This spectacular heap of ruins was once a church in Ecuador, thrown to the ground during a quake in 1949 which killed more than five thousand people.

UNESCO (Rex Keating)

while great gushes of flame shot from the land – or so the terrified inhabitants believed.

The temporary effect on water levels has been even more remarkable. An earthquake in 1158 in London was said to have dried up the River Thames so that people could walk across it, while at Baileyborough in Ireland the local lake overflowed and then subsided leaving behind on the shore "great quantities of pike and elles of prodigious size." More fanciful would appear to be an account that the River Po in Italy was so affected by an earthquake in 1173, that it was raised in the form of an arch, so that people could actually walk beneath it. Little wonder that "the approach of the Last Day was apprehended." Less fictionally, the fluctuation of water levels is considered a highly promising line of research in earthquake prediction.

Of all the watery manifestations of earthquakes it is the so-called Tidal Wave – the *tsunami*, or more correctly the seismic sea waves – which are only too often the most terrifying aspect of an earthquake to those who live near the sea. An ancient theory held that these were formidable tide races which "springing from the depths of the ocean" would advance rapidly upon sloping beaches destroying everything in their path. Mallet thought that their cause might be due to underwater slippage, and this is now believed to be the case – be it a sudden rise or sudden fall of part of the seabed. Equally, landslides, inland earthquakes, or volcanic explosions such as the monumental eruption of Krakatoa in 1883, can generate tsunamis. This eruption resulted in a succession of great waves one hundred feet (30 m)

To coast dwellers it is the tsunami, the seismic seawave – incorrectly, and usually called a tidal wave – that poses a greater threat than the tremor itself.

This shows an artist's impression of one that struck Sumatra, Indonesia in 1861.

Tsunami have occurred on many occasions in the Straits of Messina between Italy and Sicily. This ship was cast onto land near the little port of Scylla during the Calabria earthquake of 1783.

high which crossed the ocean at speeds of over 300 miles per hour (483 kmph) and hurtled onto the coasts of islands in the East Indies, causing, it was estimated, over 36,000 deaths.

It is believed that there are three types of earthquake waves which travel in water: the tsunami itself; a sound wave traveling at around 3,000 mph (4,830 kmph) which can be heard on board ships; and a mysterious wave which is not fully understood but which moves at speeds faster than sound and appears to have little effect. It is this last wave which could prove a fruitful source of early warning as it rebounds off the ionosphere (the electrified air in the upper atmosphere which reflects radio waves).

Traveling outward in concentric ripples from the underwater epicenter or source of slippage, the tsunami waves move at speeds of up to 600 mph (966 kmph). These waves can be enormous – up to 300 miles (483 km) long. To a ship at sea, the passing of a tsunami is hardly noticeable beyond a slight jar, as though a heavy box had fallen on the deck, as one sailor described it. But as the water becomes more shallow and the speed of the wave is slowed, its height increases with terrifying rapidity. If the water is confined not only by lack of depth, but also funneled by the arms of a bay or inlet, the height is magnified to an enormous extent. Its power is awe-inspiring and the damage caused as it crashes on the shore can be colossal. Sizable ships are cast up high and dry and left well inland. Substantial houses and buildings are crushed with ease. Parking meters after the great tsunami which flattened much of Hilo in Hawaii in 1946 were bent like straws.

*El mar se retira* is the age-old cry in South America that a tsunami is imminent. First the sea rises, slowly and silently to well beyond the normal high tide mark – "the smooth one" they call it. This is followed by a mighty sucking sound as the water retreats leaving rocks, reefs and sunken wrecks completely exposed while ships at anchor are stranded. Then, out to sea a phenomenon can be seen like "whales at play," their "backs" rhythmically rolling above the surface of the water as the latter becomes choppy and a fierce turbulence rolls up the sand from the ocean floor. Finally, with a terrifying noise, a huge wave traveling at a colossal speed – sometimes up to 125 mph (201 kmph) – sweeps in toward the land engulfing and swallowing everything in its path. The water remains high for some time, ten to fifteen minutes or even longer, and then with that same sucking noise the sea withdraws tearing loose anything in its course. Some time later, more waves moving at progressively slower speeds, come to finish the job.

To our ancestors in tsunami-prone areas, "tidal waves" following earthquakes were further proof of the divine hand of God, and their imaginations went to work in sheer terror. In Japan there were many tales of the crests of tsunami being fringed with ghostly lights, as the great force of the water swept up microscopic luminous organisms from the bottom and dragged them to the surface. Some accounts talk of the water "boiling" and the sight of the short, choppy sea looks indeed very like bubbling water. Others reported that men and women were "scalded" in the sea as their bodies came up covered in burns – burns caused by the rapid scrubbing action of sand particles as they were rubbed along the sea bottom and then hurled into the air in the "boiling" water. The unfortunate community of Scylla in Italy, ravaged by an inland earthquake fled to the sea, led by their prince, only to be hit by a wave reported as "boiling hot" which stormed ashore for three miles (4.8 km). This swept away, so the record says, 2,473 inhabitants, with their prince still leading them.

The tsunami that followed the great Lisbon earthquake was felt on both sides of the Atlantic. At Antigua, 3,400 miles (5,474 km) from Lisbon a remarkable tide of twelve feet (3.6 m) was reported, and the water was black; further west on the island of Saba, the sea rose a massive twenty-one feet (6.3 m), elsewhere in the West Indies tides of fifteen feet (4.5 m) or more were reported from a number of places. But in Barbados, where the tide rose to a great height people found it "utterly incredible" that their tide could have anything to do with the Lisbon earthquake when news of the disaster eventually reached them.

Nearer the epicenter at Oporto, 180 miles (289.8 km) from Lisbon, the river overflowed its banks and two of the Brazil fleet on their way to the New World were driven back. At Cadiz, on the Spanish coast 260 miles (418 km) from Lisbon, a mighty wave estimated at sixty feet (18 m) in height hurled itself upon the town. Mercifully, most of its force was spent on the stretch of rocks which protected Cadiz from the west, nevertheless, the force of the water was sufficient to break down some of the battlements and move a number of guns which weighed up to ten tons (10,170 kg). The causeway connecting the town to the mainland was completely washed away with all the people on it, including a young man called Racine, grandson of the great French dramatist. The worst damage was experienced in the River Tagus. The retreat of the sea laid bare the bar across the mouth of the river, and then, a huge wave fifty feet (15 m) high broke on the old fort of Belem. The wave tore upstream leaving devastation on the banks of the Tagus as it went. Over the lower parts of Lisbon, a wave twenty feet (6 m) high swept in over the houses and streets. Bridges were broken, walls overturned, hundreds of people drowned, and on its retreat large ships were torn from their moorings, and carried out to sea to disappear with the loss of all hands. The water rose and fell three times until, gradually, the river regained its normal level. At Gibraltar, the sea behaved in a peculiar way, rising and falling to a height of six feet (1.8 m) every quarter of an hour until well on into the next morning. In the Azores and on the island of Madeira, great quantities of fish were left high and dry when the water receded. At Kinsale on the southern coast of Ireland, one thousand miles (1,610 km) from Lisbon, a large mass of water suddenly poured into the harbor in the early afternoon without warning and swept away everything in its path. In the ports of Ireland, and up and down the south and west coasts of England, the reports were the same, with the sea rising as little as six feet (1.8 m) in some places to as much as nine feet (2.7 m) in others. The ports of Europe experienced similar treatment. In many harbors buoys as well as ships were snapped from their moorings.

The extraordinary water effect of the Lisbon earthquake clearly demonstrated the phenomenon of seiches – the effect, like water slopping in a bath or a saucer, of many small sloshing movements, in inland bodies of water or even large containers like tubs or cisterns. Angus MacDermot, an innkeeper in Tarbert in Scotland saw one of the largest seiches and, "with his watch in his hand all the time of the agitation," observed Loch Lomond suddenly and "without the least gust of wind" rising against its banks, retiring, and five minutes later subsiding. Nearby Loch Long, Loch Ness and Loch Catrine were also reported to have behaved similarly at the same time. The rise of the latter was witnessed by two workmen. "This is ominous" declared one: "It is one of the wonderful works of God," said the other. It is interesting to note that Loch Lomond is 1,300 miles (2,093 km) from Lisbon.

Japan is renowned for the tsunami which, since time immemorial, have ravaged her coastline. One in 1896 is believed to have killed over 27,000 people. Devastating tsunami have struck Japan at least fifteen times in the last three hundred years. The Japanese had a saying that you should run to the bamboos – where the matted network of roots provided a moderately stable and more-or-less earthquake-proof base – when an earthquake strikes, and run to the hills when the sea withdraws. Mercifully, it is possible using modern methods to give reasonable warning of the onset of a tsunami. In the past these warnings, either because the recipients thought they knew best or because of the lack of credibility of the system itself, often went unheeded by the curious or unwary. But education, the bitter experience of others and a greater degree of reliability in tsunami prediction has changed that.

Most of the principal islands of the Hawaiian chain are protected by reefs or the gradually rising sea bottom which absorbs the energy of the tsunami, but not Hawaii itself. The island is surrounded by very deep water, and submarine trenches lie immediately outside its principal harbors. With the water shallowing rapidly, an oncoming tsunami builds to a prodigious height and pounds down on the unprotected shores of the island.

This is what occurred as an aftermath to the great Aleutian Islands quake of 1946. Within minutes of the earthquake striking, a colossal wave one hundred feet (30 m) high swept down on the lighthouse at Scotch Cap on Unimak Island literally wiping it away with its crew of five. A little more than four hours later the wave struck Hawaii, two thousand miles (3,220 km) away. It was on the morning of April Fool's Day, and the crews of two freighters moored one mile (1.6 km) off Hilo Bay were horrified to see a mighty wall of water, which had passed them as a gentle undulation no more than four feet (1.2 m) high, suddenly rise from the ocean surface and crash

The great tsunami that struck Hawaii after the Aleutian earthquake of 1946 left a trail of devastation and a death toll of 173. This photograph, taken from a ship in harbor, shows the wave about to break at Hilo. The disaster led to the creation of the Tsunami Warning System which today monitors the passage of seismic seawaves throughout the Pacific.

James W. Duncan

upon the resort of Hilo on the eastern side of the island of Hawaii. The wave was fifty-five feet (16.5 m) high. It swept into the harbor crushing everything in its path and leaving a trail of devastation and a death toll of 173, and many injured – the worst natural disaster in the history of the island.

The disaster triggered research into the cause, and, above all, the forecasting of tsunami. Two years after the Hilo tsunami the Seismic Sea-Wave Warning System was established, the forerunner of an international network with its center at Honolulu which today spans the Pacific and gives warning of approaching tsunami.

The value of the warning system has already been amply proved. The massive tsunami which succeeded the Chilean earthquake of 1960, a quake of 9.5 magnitude, pounded shores from South America, to the Philippines and Japan with waves 15 feet to 35 feet (4.5–10.5 m) high, doing a great deal of damage. In Hawaii 61 people died, but it could have been much worse. Four years later the 9.2 magnitude Alaskan earthquake, the greatest earthquake in North American history, produced a wave 15 feet (4.5 m) high, and damage up and down the western American seaboard. But warning had been received in good time and the death toll was less than it might have been.

The network controlled from Honolulu and previously administered by the National Oceanic and Atmospheric Administration and now by the National Weather Service comprizes reporting stations in and surrounding the Pacific Ocean. When a quake of 7.5 magnitude or over occurs in the

The approaching wave. An awesome    Tuberculosis Hospital, Hawaii.
picture taken from the Putamaile                    Harry A. Simms Sr.

Pacific area the epicenter is calculated and a *Tsunami Watch* call goes out, to all stations in the network as well as to the military and civil authorities concerned. Each station in the network detects and reports the sea-waves as they pass in order to monitor the progress of the tsunami. From this data it is possible to calculate when the wave is likely to reach the many populated areas at risk around the Pacific. A tsunami produced by a quake in Alaska will reach Hawaii six or so hours later, Japan around nine hours, and the Philippines fourteen hours after the main shock. A tsunami originating off the coast of South America is likely to reach Honolulu within fifteen hours and Japan about a day after the initial tremor.

Once the timing of the tsunami has been worked out, a *Tsunami Warning* is flashed round the Pacific and the appropriate authorities can take the necessary action. The timing can be worked out to a reasonable degree of accuracy, but what cannot be calculated infallibly is whether or not a tsunami will break on the shore in the form of a massive "tidal wave" or merely as an abnormally high tide. Tsunami still have a high degree of unpredictability about them. There will inevitably be instances of over-warning, but most people in tsunami-prone areas have learned to be prepared for false alarms as well as for the big waves themselves. Soon satellite photography from a station orbiting above the international dateline will provide instant recording of tsunami propagation, and speed up the warning process.

Any warning system, though, can only be as effective as the attention paid to it. There have been cases of people wandering to the reefs or the shore to search for fish left high and dry by the receding water. Curious sightseers go to look at the strange sight of rocks and reefs laid bare by the

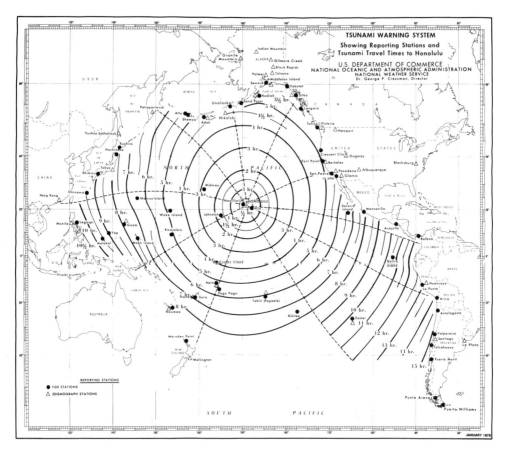

TSUNAMI WARNING SYSTEM

Showing Reporting Stations and
Tsunami Travel Times to Honolulu

U.S. DEPARTMENT OF COMMERCE
NATIONAL OCEANIC AND ATMOSPHERIC ADMINISTRATION
NATIONAL WEATHER SERVICE
Dr. George P. Cressman, Director

Reporting stations of the Tsunami Warning System now handled by the US National Weather Center, with travel times across the Pacific of a hypothetical tsunami centered on Honolulu.

International Tsunami Information Center

sea. The unhappy example is often cited of a Japanese community warned by a suddenly receding tide and fleeing to higher ground, only to be driven from there by an earthquake, and running once more to the shore only to be engulfed by a tsunami. In the early days, there were so many false alarms that people came to look on the operation as little more than a scare machine. The system has now achieved credibility and a warning time of several hours is now the norm. The tsunami has been robbed of much of its mystery.

The effects of an earthquake on water are remarkable, and can be alarming; the secondary effects on land can be as pronounced. These include landslides and avalanches, drops or uplifts, and fractures or pressure ridges. Fissures sometimes develop, and to many this aspect is the most frightening – to see the solid earth suddenly open out, threatening to swallow man and beast. In the Port Royal earthquake of 1692, a story is told of a man engulfed in a giant fissure only to be thrown out at the next violent tremor of the earth. Reports of these experiences are often unreliable. A cow was supposedly caught in a fissure resulting from the San Francisco earthquake of 1906 with only its tail protruding, but when observers went to verify the reports the animal had disappeared and it is believed the whole story was a myth.

Permanent horizontal or vertical displacement is more common. After the same 1906 earthquake there was as much as a twenty-foot (6 m) shifting in some areas and many examples of smaller displacement. The 1952 Kern County, California earthquake produced a vertical movement of two feet (0.6 m); the 1971 quake at San Fernando led to displacements of six feet (1.8 m) vertically, and the same distance horizontally.

Subsidence, liquefaction – when the soil loses all cohesion and becomes a soggy, muddy mass – uplift, and tilting are all phenomena associated with the after-effects of earthquakes, but few have resulted in quite so remarkable an alteration to the landscape as that which took place at New Madrid, Missouri, in the Mississippi Valley in 1811 and 1812.

At two A.M. on December 16, 1811, the people of New Madrid were suddenly woken by the noise of creaking timbers and the crash of falling chimneys and furniture. They rushed out panic-stricken into the night, as the ground heaved and shook and their houses disintegrated under a succession of shocks. Dawn revealed an astonishing sight, and as they watched, the whole landscape heaved and swelled in long, low billows, while beneath them the ground grumbled and murmured.

The movement started great landslides. Huge slabs of cliff with hundreds of trees slid with a shattering roar into the river. Trees in the forests swung from side to side until their branches became entwined. A certain Mr. Walker was returning through the forest when the quake struck. Feeling the ground disappearing beneath his feet he sank to his knees beseeching the Almighty to desist. His companion, a Frenchman, had greater presence of mind. "Monsieur Valkare, Monsieur Valkare," he exclaimed, "this is no time to pray! Sacre Dieu! gardez-vous les branches!"

Elsewhere, great parallel fissures opened in the ground, mainly narrow and running in a northwesterly–southeasterly direction. People placed timber at right angles to the fissures and rode over these makeshift bridges. This saved many lives.

On the Mississippi, huge waves developed which overturned boats and left others high and dry. Thousands of trees were broken off, crashed into the water and eventually floated toward the sea. In a number of places faults ran across the river itself creating waterfalls and rapids. One near New Madrid itself was estimated to have been six feet (1.8 m) high and could be clearly heard. Elsewhere whole islands disappeared. It was this that probably saved the life of one family.

A certain Captain Sarpy of New Orleans was in a boat with his wife, children and a considerable sum of money. He tied up on an island not far from Vicksburg, only to spot a party of pirates waiting to rob him. Quietly he dropped downstream and moored there. To his considerable surprise when he returned the next morning there were no robbers; indeed there was no island. Everything had disappeared during the night.

The shocks continued for the next two days, at increasing intervals but diminishing intensity except for a massive shock eight weeks after the initial tremor. Records show that these shocks continued for the next couple of years.

Fortunately the area was sparsely populated. Only one man was officially reported killed when his house collapsed on top of him in New Madrid. However, the town was a total wreck and was never rebuilt. The shocks of the New Madrid quakes were felt over a vast area. Missouri, Arkansas, Kentucky and Tennessee all experienced damage of one sort or another. In Washington, D.C., the tremor was so bad that people were very frightened. In Boston, 1,100 miles (1,771 km) away, the shaking was quite distinctive, and people in southern Canada were also mildly affected. The New Madrid earthquake is best known for its effect on the landscape, however. Astonishing changes were made. The Tiptonville Dome, fifteen miles (24.2 km) long by eight miles (13 km) wide was elevated to a height of twenty feet (6 m) in places. New bodies of water were created at Lake Saint Francis in Arkansas – forty miles (65 km) long by half-a-mile (0.8 km) wide – and at Reelfoot Lake in Tennessee. Reelfoot Lake was shallow, the depth varying between five (1.5 m) and twenty feet (6 m), and full of submerged trees which died when the water level was raised so dramatically. These strange skeletons were left

Reelfoot Lake. An artificial lake created by the New Madrid, Missouri, earthquake of 1811.

USGS (M.L. Fuller)

as gaunt reminders of the great natural catastrophe.

In some places, jets of sand, mud or gas occurred. Sand blows, like great potters' wheels eight to fifteen feet (2.4–4.5 m) across, white against the black alluvial sand and distinctive like crazy checkers appeared over a huge area. Sand depressions, three to five feet (0.9–1.5 m) wide, soon filled with water and formed long narrow pools.

James Audubon, the naturalist, was riding through Kentucky at the time. He later described his experiences, "the ground rose and fell in successive furrows like the ruffled waters of a lake. . . . The earth waved like a field of corn before the breeze." Seven years after the tremors another visitor described the country as having "a melancholy aspect of chasms, of sand covering the earth, of trees thrown down or lying at an angle of forty-five degrees, or split in the middle." Some trees were indeed literally neatly split down the middle, and growing, apparently without much harm, on either side of a fissure. Nearly 230 square miles (595 sq km) of forest was believed to be lost.

The Alaskan earthquake of 1958 caused an enormous landslide into Lituya Bay which generated a wave surging to 1,720 feet (524 m) up the mountainside. The rockslide occurred at upper left of the picture and caused total destruction of forest over the light areas. NOAA/EDS

Although the upper Mississippi and Ohio Valleys suffer quite frequent earthquakes, nothing in the United States has ever matched the New Madrid quakes in either extent or severity. The cause is believed to have been the New Madrid fault which runs in a northeast–southwest direction, but to those who experienced it, the cause was supernatural and beyond reason. One man thought that a comet with two horns had passed. Earth had successfully rolled over one of the horns, but the struggle to surmount the second was more difficult and as earth tried so she shook in her endeavors. With a note of profound gloom the author announced that if earth was successful all would be well, but if not . . . then the end of the world was nigh.

Another reckoned that the cause of the quakes was due to a great layer of driftwood which passed under the Mississippi Valley. A man called James MacFarlane presented a paper to the American Association for the Advancement of Science with the provocative title *The Earthquake at New Madrid in 1811, probably not an Earthquake*. He came to this conclusion on the grounds that the disturbance was due to subsidence; that no great alluvial region had ever been struck by an earthquake before; and finally, that earthquakes do not occur so far from the seashore!

Although the land effects of the New Madrid quake were stupendous, lesser tremors have also been responsible for large-scale earth moving.

In 1571 an amazed witness of an earthquake in Herefordshire, England described the movement of a prominent hill called Marclay Hill: "With a roaring noise [it] remov'd itself from the place where it stood, and for three days together travell'd from its Old Seat. It began first to take its Journey February 17, being Saturday, at six of the Clock at Night, and by seven next morning it had gone forty Paces, carrying with it Sheep in their Cotes, Hedgerows and Trees . . . some that stood upon the Plain, are firmly growing upon the Hill; those that were East turned West, and those in the West were set in the East . . . continuing for four hundred Yards leaving Pasturage in places of the Tillages, and the Tillage overpressed with Pasturage." It finally went up a hill "twelve fathoms high and there rested after three days travel."

Landslides are a frequent occurrence in California. Over the last ten years, there have been four thousand of them in the Los Angeles basin alone. Fortunately none have been as spectacular as that which resulted from the Good Friday earthquake in Alaska in 1964, the greatest earthquake ever recorded in North America, registering 9.2 on the Richter scale.

The epicenter of the earthquake was twelve miles (19.3 km) under Prince William Sound off the coast of Alaska. It was 5.36 P.M. when the earthquake struck with no warning. For a full three to four minutes, the ground rolled and lurched. Cars were literally bounced off the roads, huge fissures opened in the streets, and the greatest crustal deformation ever known took place with astonishing rapidity. The area of damage was estimated at 50,000 square miles (129,500 sq km); the area which felt the earthquake was com-

At Anchorage, the Alaskan earthquake of 1964 led to remarkable ground deformation. At Turnagain Heights the land folded, fissured and fell away leaving many houses like this one tilted at a crazy angle.    NOAA/EDS

The Alaskan quake also snapped off these trees like matchwood at heights from 88 feet (27 m) to 101 feet (31 m) above low water at Shoup Bay.

USGS (G. Plafker)

A monumental landslide followed the earthquake in Peru in 1970. An avalanche about 1,000 yards wide (914.4 m) and one mile (1.61 km) long swept down the slope at a speed estimated at 100 mph (160.94 kmph). Containing some 80 million cubic feet of water, mud and rocks it killed more than twenty thousand people in the towns of Yungay and Ronrahirca, which lie under this chaos of boulders

puted at half a million square miles (1.3 million sq km). Well levels in South Africa fluctuated violently. Waves four feet (1.2 m) high broke on the shore of the Gulf of Mexico. An atmospheric wave was felt up to two thousand miles (3,220 km) away. The earthquake was responsible for 115 deaths, and it all but crippled Alaska's economy. But the most spectacular effects were felt on the coastline.

In the port of Valdez, the old converted liberty ship, SS *Chena*, was discharging cargo when the quake struck. She rose twenty to thirty feet (6–9 m), bottomed, rose again, bottomed, and then lifted clear, all in the space of a few incredible minutes. Thanks to an instantaneous response from the engine room, the *Chena* struggled clear, through the remains of what had once been a cannery and found open water. She was none the worse.

The *Chena* was more fortunate than those on shore. The skipper saw the dock at Valdez literally break in two and then vanish. People on it started to run, but by then it was too late – they had nowhere to run to. Four waves in all struck Valdez, but these were due to landslides which hit the water and caused a series of giant seiches.

The port of Seward experienced a monumental landslip as tons of shore slid into the bay. As the ground gently subsided, it took with it much of the Standard Oil tank farm, and as the tanks slid toward the sea, they ruptured and exploded with a roar, sending flames into the air two hundred feet (60 m) high. Further inland lay the Texaco Oil tank farm, and on the connecting rail track was a long line of eighty freight cars. These caught fire one by one in a chain reaction which crept remorselessly nearer the Texaco tanks themselves. Soon they too exploded in a blast of black smoke and darting flame.

At Resurrection Bay, the normally placid water was disturbed by incredible turbulence as water rebounded from one side of the narrow inlet to the other. Most people rushed to the only high ground nearby, where the hospital was situated, to wait for the tsunami, which they knew must come. Others tried to drive to safety on the only road from the shattered community.

The tsunami finally came thirty minutes after the initial shock. It was a great wave thirty feet (9 m) high, which picked up burning oil as it came down the narrow waterway to approach what had once been the waterfront of Seward. It was fringed with burning debris, and this soon blocked the only road from the stricken town. In all, three waves struck Seward, but by the time the last, and biggest, hit the town, anything movable had been swept into the water.

Anchorage, however, suffered the greatest damage, and remarkably there was no tsunami, only a massive landslide.

Other spectacular ground movements have been recorded in many parts of the world after or during earthquakes. At Riocamba, Chile in 1797 sailors witnessed the ground appearing to rise before their very eyes, and to add a macabre touch, the local graveyard was suddenly laid bare and tombs rose to the surface to reveal dozens of sitting skeletons gazing out to sea like ghostly sentinels. The movement in this earthquake appears to have been extraordinary. "The earth evidently moved round like a fluid in streams or currents," described a highly puzzled observer. First the ground appeared to sink, then to run horizontally and finally upward. Houses and buildings were squashed and crushed. Sorting out ownership of belongings in the turmoil that resulted involved years of legal wrangling.

The physical effects of an earthquake are bad enough, but the psychological effects are just as profound. Medical men are worried by the extent and duration of psychological damage from disasters.

If material damage can be catastrophic,   in an earthquake in Iran.
damage in human terms can be vastly
greater. These are children orphaned        League of Red Cross Societies

The phenomenon is not new. Sir William Hamilton, in his report on the Calabrian earthquakes of 1783, paints a vivid picture of disaster and dismay: "I travelled four days in the plain in the midst of such misery as cannot be described," he wrote. "The force of the earthquake was so great there, that all the inhabitants of the towns were buried either alive or dead under the ruins of their houses in an instant." For those still alive, "even the braying of an ass, the neighing of a horse, or the cackling of a goose drove people outside in panic." In the country, "the people expected the earth to open up and swallow them whole."

During this earthquake, Messina in Sicily, so often destroyed in the past, was once again wrecked. Here, however, Hamilton notes that the nuns were walking about under the eyes of their confessor and seemed gay, enjoying the freedom which the earthquake had given them, as indeed were the schoolboys, and he notes, half-humorously, that earthquakes are "particularly pleasing" to nuns and schoolboys. More seriously, he observes throughout his journey, "a prevailing indolence, inactivity, and want of spirit, which is unfortunate, as such a heavy and general calamity can only be repaired by a disposition directly contrary to that."

This is much in line with what prospectors noticed about the victims of the Yakatut earthquake in Alaska in 1899. Here, the strange, pallid and frightened look which people had was dubbed the "earthquake face."

Physically, giddiness is frequently felt during an earthquake, and

"There were no tears, it was beyond tears." This old lady, the only surviving member of her family after an earthquake, seems oblivious even of the rosary or the compassion offered her.

The Times

headaches can also result. "A strong apprehension of the heart" was noticed by one man, "a kind of gasping anxiety, weakness in the limbs, and a slight sickness in the stomach." One who witnessed the London earthquake reckoned that the earthquake affected all those of weak nerves, or who had a nervous complaint. It was, so he thought, obnoxious to hysterics, colics, rheumatic pains, and could affect people with shortness of breath. Others felt pins and needles in their joints, but some actually found that their rheumatism was cured or improved, while one man after the Charleston earthquake who had been abnormally nervous and depressed, reacted immediately to the shock therapy of the earthquake and became his normal self soon after.

It has been found that 50 percent of survivors suffer from some neurosis after a catastrophe like an earthquake. They appear listless, without sense of purpose, and it is essential to keep them occupied immediately after the disaster. And these effects may last for years. Even after the lapse of two years since the Bucharest earthquake of March 1977, a child who was then three, still reacts to sudden noise. Should a particularly noisy truck pass the door she will instinctively run to hold on to a table or another piece of heavy furniture. And others who have experienced earthquakes say that it may take three or four years for all the effects to wear off.

Nightmares, many centered on falling, are frequently reported afterward, as well as acute guilt complexes. There is an increase in divorce, but close families often become closer still, as if bonded by the sharing of a terrifying experience. Initially, when disaster strikes, an elemental instinct for self-preservation overrides everything else, and most people grasp whatever is nearest and rush to where they think safety lies. If children or other close family members are abandoned, even for a short while, extreme feelings of guilt often occur after the earthquake is over. It has been estimated that only 25 percent of the population will "keep their heads" in such a disaster – the remainder will need direction and some sense of immediate purpose. After the earthquake, reassurance and some type of order are very important. In these situations, the presence of volunteer organizations can have great psychological as well as practical importance. Disaster training is also invaluable.

However, it seems that there is no real way of preparing mentally for a great disaster. Many people will panic, and do things, which on sober reflection they would never do. One group of Europeans found that too much composure almost cost them their lives in a South American earthquake. While everyone around them went to pieces, they remained calm, and somewhat aloof, until one distraught native noticed them. "Look at those heretics," he cried, "they will not even get out of their beds!" They got up then, and in a hurry.

Of all the secondary effects following an earthquake, it is fire which has cost more lives and damage than any other factor. Fire ravaged the ruins of Lisbon; completed the destruction of San Francisco after the earthquake of 1906; and raged unchecked through Kingston, Jamaica the following year. Fire was also the crowning catastrophe of the 1923 Kanto Plain earthquake in Japan – the greatest natural disaster the country has ever experienced in modern times.

On the eastern coast of Honshu, the central of the three main islands which comprise the Japanese archipelago, and south of the capital Tokyo, and the thriving port of Yokohama, lies the great Kanto Plain. Bordered on the west and the south by the highlands of central Honshu, and on the seaward side

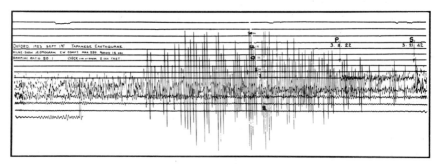

How the seismograph at Oxford, England recorded the great Kanto Plain earthquake of 1923 in Japan.
Science Museum

by the majestic sweep of Sagami Bay, it was here, in an area ninety miles by fifty miles (145 by 80.5 km) that the main geological effects of the great earthquake of 1923 occurred.

In Japanese mythology, September 1 is a day to be wary of, a day of premonition, and the morning of September 1, 1923, a Saturday, was remembered as being stifling and airless in Tokyo, while in Yokohama, twenty-five miles (40.3 km) to the south, there was a glaring sun and a strong, shifting breeze. Workers in both cities were looking forward to the weekend and leaving work punctually at noon. Already many had left for the seaside resort of Kamakura on Sagami Bay. Of the large European business community, a number were seeing off friends who were sailing that afternoon in the Canadian Pacific liner the *Empress of Australia* bound for Vancouver, others were putting the finishing touch to the week's business in their offices, many of which were located near the waterfront.

Then, precisely seventy-six seconds before noon, three shocks of incredible intensity struck the Kanto Plain. It was calculated that there were 171 aftershocks during the next six hours, but the three main shocks were enough to wreck the two cities. Suddenly, and with incredible finality, two great communities were snuffed out.

An officer on a ship wrote later: "A yellow cloud very thin at first but growing in size every second rose from the land, from behind the houses, the docks, the hills beyond. This cloud formed a continuous strip all around the bay, growing in size and deepening in colour, travelling at great speed towards the north."

Professor Akitsume Imamura of the Imperial University was in his seismological laboratory at the moment of the shocks. With exemplary scientific detachment he recorded his impressions: "At first the movement was rather slow so I did not take it as the forerunner of so big a shock. As usual I began to estimate the duration of the preliminary tremors and determined if possible the direction of the principal movements. . . . Seven or eight seconds passed and the building was shaking to an extraordinary extent, but I considered these movements not yet to be the principal portion. At the twelfth second from the start, according to my calculation, came a very big vibration which I took to be the beginning of the principal motion. Now the motion instead of becoming less and less as usual, went on increasing in intensity very quickly, and after four or five seconds I felt it to have reached its strongest. During this epoch the tiles were showering down from the roof, making a loud noise, and I wondered whether the building could stand or not. . . . For the next few minutes we felt an undulating movement like we experience on a boat in windy weather." The professor and his assistants stayed at their post, continuing to take observations and putting out a fire which threatened their building. Four of them lost their houses in the holocaust knowing that their families were in jeopardy.

On the Kanto Plain huge fissures appeared in the ground. The wooden pillars supporting a bridge which had been built in 1182, across the Sagami River, reappeared miraculously after an absence of nearly 750 years. The pipes which lined the walls used by the farmers were pushed out of the ground to the extent of ten feet (3 m), and left sticking incongruously above the fields like monstrous pins on a giant cribbage board. Great landslides altered the landscape drastically and permanently, and then in Sagami Bay a tsunami gathered strength and in a mighty wave, thirty-four feet (10.2 m) high in places, with many subsequent smaller ones, swept over the coast. An estimated one hundred people bathing in the little horseshoe-shaped bay of the resort of Kamakura and unable to escape the waters in time, were swept away and drowned. An entire train with two hundred more was caught by a landslide and swept into the middle of Sagami Bay and disappeared forever – no trace of the train was ever found and only one passenger survived. But it was in the two great cities that the most devastation was caused and one of the worst disasters in history took place.

Henry W. Kinney, author and magazine editor, was heading for Kamakura with an English friend when they were told that the train they were traveling on could go no further. They got out and walked until they reached the bridge over the Tamagawa River.

Yokohama, 1923. The quay where relatives and friends were seeing off passengers on the liner *Empress of Australia* sank at both ends, leaving cars and those on it stranded. A remarkable picture of the scene in Yokohama Bay after the earthquake and before fire wiped out the city.

Illustrated London News

Kinney wrote, "The massive buttresses supporting the railway bridge . . . had been twisted, rocked out of place and the tracks hung fantastically suspended between them. Oddly, a slight footbridge, formed by two widths of boards, was almost intact. We hurried across, the one thought in control being: what if another shock should catch us on this bridge?"

Kinney and his friend carried on, astonished at what they saw. "It seemed impossible that any inanimate manifestation of nature could be so insanely malicious as was the shock which smote Kawasaki, a large village just on the Yokohama side of the river. The houses, most of them two-storied, frail wooden structures with paper windows, crowned with roofs of heavy tiles, had not only been smashed, but had been torn apart, rended into splintered beams and raveled and torn fragments of boards jumbled together, as if they had been battered by a gigantic flail. They had been thrown in every direc-

Land movement and fissures occurred
in many places in the Kanto Plain.                    Illustrated London News

tion, backwards, against each other, into the streets. The most diabolical intent could have produced no more stupendous result."

"I came," he wrote, "to the sickening realisation that there could be safety nowhere." A sugar factory was no more than a "mound of bricks, a huge confused pile and with great beams and splintered wood protruding haphazardly." The rest was in flames. While further on a large ferro-concrete building was smashed "like a battered pasteboard box." Approaching Yokohama, the damage appeared to be even more intense. Mud walls topped with thatch had collapsed as if some huge pressure had suddenly squashed them flat. The only way to travel was over the roofs.

The triple shock brought every building of consequence in Yokohama to the ground. Wreckage was total. Tokyo was in little better shape. Although uptown parts of the city whose foundations rested on rock were hardly affected, downtown Tokyo, built on alluvial soil was almost obliterated. But already the menace which was to demolish most of what was left of the two cities was mustering its forces.

With thousands of Japanese preparing their midday meal for husbands and families returning from their half-day's work, the tremors had overset innumerable cooking stoves and charcoal braziers. In an instant many of the matchbox houses were a mass of flame, and fanned by the wind, the flames merged to become an inferno. The terrified population, carrying on their heads whatever they could lay their hands on – often, disastrously, bedding or *futons* (padded quilts) – rushed hither and thither as fire blocked all escape routes. Soon, in a hundred instances, falling sparks and debris set alight to the precious loads which became flaming torches to spread the fire. The tremors had also shaken off many tin roofs exposing the wooden beams beneath to flying sparks and flame.

Within minutes the fires were wholly out of control. In Tokyo, water supplies were cut off. The efforts of the firemen who, regardless of risk, carried on with their hopeless task, using long hoses from canals and ditches, managed to extinguish a few fires, but the task was impossible.

Then, with an awful malignancy, starting in the upper reaches of the Samida River, which flows through the center of Tokyo, the wind, which had been variable all morning, became what the Japanese aptly call the *taksumaki* – the dragon's twist – a cyclone which at four in the afternoon headed for the city. Hurtling forward at an estimated speed of 125 mph (201.3 kmph) it bore down on Tokyo. Boats were lifted bodily into the air, the water sucked up in a huge muddy column, and then it struck the blazing city. Snatching burning timbers, furniture, clothing, even bodies upward into the sky, the cyclone hurled them down again to spread the fire even further. Tokyo became an inferno. Nearly three-quarters of the entire city was wiped out, the fire burned for two whole days until there was nothing left to burn and left the blackened shell of what had been Japan's proud capital city.

As fire bore down on them, completely out of hand and seemingly from all directions, the people of Tokyo rushed for the open spaces. One was a ten-acre (0.04 sq km) area formerly the Military Clothing Depot and now an empty, open space, in a suburb called Honjo. Here a huge crowd of people gathered in terrified awe; while all around the fire raged. Then, as though carefully guided by a hidden hand, the cyclone bore down on the Clothing Depot. In an instant a firestorm of incredible ferocity had built up. The air was parched. Bodies, clothes and houses dehydrated in an instant. The heat was so intense that people's hair, their clothing, their tinder-dry bodies caught fire. It was estimated that 40,000 people, men, women, children, entire families and all they possessed were engulfed in one roaring mass of flames and were roasted alive. There were just thirty survivors.

Yokohama was hardly better off, for here the quake had fractured a number of oil storage tanks. The oil swept down the many drains igniting on the way until it reached the waterfront which was soon ablaze from end to end, and the flames were fanned by a steady onshore wind. Kinney, having reached some high ground overlooking the port, described the whole lurid panorama spread beneath him, "It was meaningless – there were no landmarks, no familiar buildings from which one might determine locality. Yokohama the city of almost half a million souls, had become a vast plain of fire, of red, devouring sheets of flame which played and flickered. . . ." One moment "I had faced a city of square mile on square mile of houses, great office-buildings, banks, hotels, stores, houses, and when I turned back again, it had vanished, as if by some gigantic sweep of malevolent magic . . . and all over were people, people one knew, whom one had danced with, dined with, played bridge with, reduced in a moment to the uttermost depth of despair, standing, crying wildly, by the ruins, clawing at them desperately, to reach others caught under the bricks, and already, here and there, the flames were leaping forth, coming closer and closer, while the poor wretches in the debris were yelling for help." Another man, a Japanese journalist wrote with shattering poignancy, "I am a newspaperman, and I've been thinking how I'm going to write this. Phrases and images, monstrous incidents that have flickered before me all this afternoon, are running in my mind haphazard; but I can't do it. It can't be done. It's too viciously, demoniacally monstrous."

In Yokohama, whirlwinds did what the cyclone had done in Tokyo. The bridges connecting the many parts of Yokohama had been destroyed by the earthquake. On what were now islands, people huddled at the mercy of the blazing inferno which swept on to and through each isolated piece of the city in turn. Some fleeing from the flames hurled themselves into the water, to perish by drowning. Some people rushed into the water at the Bund, ducking when the heat became too intense. Others found boats anchored in the shallows, and they too were caught up in the conflagration.

Refugees crowded the five hills behind the port, as well as Yokohama

Park. Here the fire billowed back and forth raining burning debris on the survivors. A burst water main had flooded part of the spacious park and in a waist-deep swamp the fortunate ones huddled protecting themselves from falling cinders. A Swiss merchant later wrote, "We crouched in it and tore off our clothes to cover our heads and faces against the heat." Others watched in horrified fascination as their neighbors burst into flames before their eyes and became raging pyres – wet mud saved some, but not many. In the middle of the night, the Swiss merchant heard a voice calling in English, "I am here to save you folk." It was an officer from the *Empress of Australia*, who led the half-dead survivors to safety.

The final death toll was never known, but more than 100,000 people were killed or declared missing, while a further 50,000 suffered from injuries of varying severity. (The atom bomb at Hiroshima killed 80,000, but a further 40,000 died later from residual radioactivity.) A more terrifying statistic was that only seven people in every hundred out of the entire population of Yokohama *escaped* injury. Little the wonder that the official Japanese report on the great earthquake records, "The disaster was really the most horrible ever known since authentic history began."

# 5
# When Disaster Strikes

FOR THREE DAYS the fire raged unchecked in Lisbon. "The prospect of the city was deplorable," described one survivor, "as you passed along the streets you saw shops of goods with the shopkeepers buried with them. Some alive crying out from under the ruins, others half buried, others with broken limbs, in vain begging for help. . . . In the fields, where, if you happened to forget yourself with sleep, you were awakened by the tremblings of the earth and the howlings of the people."

While the population of Lisbon found sanctuary outside the city, the lawless went to work among the ruins, robbing the dead, killing the injured for their rings and jewelry, breaking into the rubble-strewn shells of buildings seeking treasure and riches.

A state of total lawlessness was imminent, but one man rose above the chaos and restored order amid the carnage and ruin. This was Sebastião de Carvalho, later the Marquês de Pombal, secretary of state to the Portuguese king. Miraculously, his house had been spared by the quake. People thought that this was a divine indication that Carvalho had been chosen to save the capital city. As soon as he could, Carvalho hastened by carriage to nearby Belem, where the king and royal family were in a state of considerable alarm, surrounded by priests who pointed out, somewhat unkindly, that none of this would have happened had it not been for the monarch's own manifold sins. The only recourse now, they said, was for him to pray for belated forgiveness.

Into this condition of near-hysteria, Carvalho appeared like a ministering angel. He greeted his master's desperate plea, "What can be done? What can be done to meet this infliction of Divine Justice?" with words which have gone down in Portuguese history, "Sire," he replied, "We must bury the dead and feed the living." For the next three days Carvalho lived in his coach, subsisting on bowls of broth brought to him by his wife, while he saw to the rescue of Lisbon, issued proclamations and directed affairs.

The fire had burned itself out by now, but the embers were still hot to the touch and an Englishman could write three weeks after the earthquake, "There are no sign of Streets, Lanes, Squares, etc., but Hill and Mountains

The ruins of Lisbon after the earthquake of 1755, the greatest in recent European history, whose effects were felt from Norway to Switzerland and across the Atlantic to the West Indies. British Museum

of Rubbish still smoaking," and he computes that hardly three thousand of the twenty thousand odd houses in Lisbon were safe enough to live in without fundamental repair. And the colossal task of clearing the rubble was further hindered as even sixteen days after the fire, the rubbish was so hot that it set the baskets carrying it on fire.

While the rest of Europe pondered on the great event of November 1, Lisbon, rising from the ashes and rubble, began to come to her battered senses. The task was massive, and there was constant fear of a second calamity. Carvalho was forced to appeal to the Patriarch to discourage his priests from further terrifying the already terrified people of Lisbon with more dire warnings of God's wrath to come, and from spreading rumors to the chancelleries of Europe that the islands of the Azores and Madeira had been entirely swallowed up.

Carvalho brought all available soldiers in from outside the city, to put out the remaining fires and then to set about re-establishing law and order. Working in from the outside, troops converged on the center of the city. As they moved slowly inward over the rubble and ruin that had been Lisbon, they arrested the looters, hanging those caught in the act on the spot to discourage the others. The magistrates were given special powers to get what help they could find from able-bodied men in their districts – if necessary in chains. A number of the fires had been started deliberately. One man boasted on the gallows that he had set fire to the king's palace and only regretted that he had failed to burn all the royal family with it.

As the city reeled from aftershocks and much of it burned to the ground in the subsequent inferno, the terrified people of Lisbon took to the fields and hills beyond the ruins.
British Museum

The entrance to the River Tagus was blockaded and every ship searched, for those who had come ashore looted what they could find and then returned laden with their booty. The offenders were arrested, brought ashore and mercilessly dealt with. At the same time, stock was taken of the food aboard the ships; excess food was confiscated and paid for. Profiteering was a capital offence. Food was brought in from outside the city and sold at the old rates. The consequences were bad for those who hoped to profit from the misery of the people by asking exorbitant prices.

The plight of the people of Lisbon was pitiful. That first night they lay in the fields outside the city, frightened, with no other protection than the clothes they wore. It was very cold, and a gentle rain came to add to their misery. Food was scarce. At first, there was no organized attempt to feed the starving population. Foreigners fled to their consulates or tried to stay with their fellow countrymen, as much for safety, if they were Protestants, as for companionship. The English consul wrote that he was beseiged by "miserable objects among the lower sort of His Majesty's subjects, who fly also to Me for Bread, and lie scattered up and down in my Garden, with their Wives and Children."

Under Carvalho's direction, however, ovens and soup kitchens were set up, and water provided. (The aqueducts had been broken by the quake.) Places were set by for any valuables found in the rubble and put under armed guard. As soon as possible, instructions were issued to start counting the human cost of the disaster, parish by parish. The dead, though, were a threat to all living. It was winter, but the risk of disease was high and it was inevitable that it would be some time before all the bodies could be found.

When corpses were discovered, they were taken out in barges to the mouth of the Tagus and sunk.

Massive international aid was offered. The British House of Commons voted a sum of £100,000 in cash, as well as food, shoes, pickaxes, shovels and crowbars. The king of Spain sent four waggons full of gold. The Senate in Hamburg promised cargoes of timber and planks. The king of France waited to hear the report of the ambassador, but instructed to him to offer all necessary aid.

Lisbon rose again.

> I saw fair Lisbon's Turrets rise,
> Her Sons revive in glad Surprize,
>    Her Fields, her Vallies bloom;
> Her Merchandize again abound,
> Again her verdant Gardens crown'd
>    With native rich Perfume.
>
> Again the temp'rate Ocean flow'd,
> Again their Fleet triumphant rode,
>    In plenteous Traffiick gay!
> Again, behold, the rising Gale
> Propitious, fills the swelling Sail,
>    And whitens all the Sea.

Modern Lisbon still shows the marks of Carvalho's genius. There was no question but that Lisbon must be rebuilt and in the same place. It was as much a matter of pride as economics. Carvalho took advantage of this unique opportunity. Broad throughfares were created, forty feet (12 m) wide, so that a central stretch would be unencumbered by the ruins of fallen buildings, clear for rescue and a sanctuary for survivors. The streets would have a pavement, a new idea from London, where a place for pedestrians was marked off by small pillars – a forerunner of the sidewalk. The architectural style known as "Pombaline" which graces much of Lisbon to this day, was the legacy left behind. Simple elegant facades, regular windows and stonework washed in pink, ochre or dark red are monuments to the savior of Lisbon.

It was a long time before the people of Lisbon recovered from their experience. Some years after the great quake, a sudden panic ensued in a bull-ring not far from Lisbon, when pickpockets shouted that they felt the first tremors of a mighty earthquake. They stole a lot of money from the terrified spectators as they stormed the exits.

On the fourth day of the fire in San Francisco, rain at last began to fall, and by Sunday morning the task of bringing the blackened, ruined shell of the city back to order began in earnest. If Lisbon owed its resurrection and survival to Carvalho, San Francisco owed hers to two men: the mayor,

Eugene Schmitz and the local army commander, Brigadier General Funston – even if subsequent examination showed that they had behaved in a high-handed manner. Schmitz, a forceful and tactless man, was disliked by many, despised by more, and distrusted by most, and two years after the great disaster he was convicted of graft and extortion. Yet he was the mayor, and San Francisco owed an unrepayable debt to him for his exemplary handling of the greatest catastrophe to hit the West Coast of America.

As soon as the quake struck and it was possible to appreciate the dimension of the calamity that had hit the beautiful city, Mayor Schmitz summoned a fifty-man relief committee of prominent citizens. Many of these were his enemies but under his leadership the committee got down to the work of saving what they could of their city. As the fire crept toward where they were holding their day and night sessions, they packed up and moved like nomads to another makeshift office, until the fire approached and drove them out again to seek temporary shelter elsewhere. Throughout, they co-ordinated the rescue operation, fighting the fire, saving life and, where they could, saving the city.

Brigadier General Funston, from his house overlooking the city on Nob Hill, had witnessed San Francisco collapse before his eyes. Soldier, explorer, journalist, botanist and experienced guerilla fighter, he immediately realized that facing him was a catastrophe of shattering dimensions. On his own initiative he ordered the army in, at first to help fight the fires, then to help rescue the trapped and help the injured. After summoning all the troops in the area to converge on San Francisco, he informed Washington of what he had done. For his contribution to saving the city, Funston was promoted to General. For the rest of his life he was blamed for the excesses and excessive zeal showed by his men under conditions no one had ever experienced before.

The first proclamation issued by the committee of fifty was one threatening to shoot looters on sight. Almost before the tremors had ceased, shops were being looted, the dead and injured being robbed of their jewelry and rings in the streets. The on-lookers, when they had overcome their initial shock, in many cases turned on the thieves, and more than one was lynched on the spot. The quick arrival of Funston's men put a stop to the worst vandalism. Looters were shot out of hand. A soldier noticed a man taking a long time to kiss goodbye to a corpse in the street, which he assumed to be a relative. When he realized the man was really going about the macabre business of chewing off the ear-rings of the dead woman, the thief was shot. Elsewhere in the town, men from the docks raided the wholesale liquor stores along the waterfront, and collapsed dead drunk in the streets or in the stores, where they were burned to death by the advancing fires.

Although troops maintained order, martial law was not declared, and it was never needed. In the end it was the good sense of the San Franciscans which did much to lessen the impact of the catastrophe. The earthquake at

"A sea of liquid fire lay beneath us. The sky above it seemed to burn at white heat, deepening into gold and orange and spread into a fierce glare." Astonished spectators in Sacramento Street watch the advancing fire. (One

San Francisco was also a shining example of what can be done in an orderly community to minimize the effects. The results would have been much worse had it not been for the plain commonsense of the ordinary citizen.

Even amid the tragedy, people found time to laugh and to compare notes. Those who had only lost their possessions considered themselves lucky, and said so. There was commiseration, compassion, and courtesy.

"How did you come out?" a newspaperman asked one refugee. "Oh, losers," she said gaily, "there ain't any winners in this game." In one open space, an elderly gentleman was cooking a meal on a homemade stove. "You will observe," he said with dignity, "that my oven is built of the best Philadelphia building brick. I scorn the common red article."

of a series of magnificent photographs
taken by Arnold Genthe during the
San Francisco earthquake of 1906).

California Historical Society

---

Makeshift shelters of all kinds started to make their appearance. "Camp de Bum" said one, "Rooms to let – on the Roof." Dwellings with names such as Hotel St. Francis or Camp Contentment caught the indomitable spirit of the place. San Francisco was in ruins, but the worst was over.

Now they set about the massive task of rebuilding their lives and their city. Helpers from outside commented on the resilience of the San Franciscans, their ingenuity in making the best of what little they had left, of their community spirit, selfless devotion and kindness to complete strangers. In its moment of disaster the city found a common bond and cohesion which no one imagined had existed. The motto which a stallholder put up outside his new makeshift business premises "Make the best of it. Fight the rest of it," exemplified the spirit of San Francisco. The phoenix rising from the flames which was added to the city seal, was a gesture of defiance, and it was also a sign of justified pride.

Tales of courage, of adventure, even of a kind of macabre humor abounded. One man fleeing from the fire shut himself in the enormous icebox at the back of his store, and remained there for several days, eventually being released more dead than alive. The story was repeated of the devotion of the priest of St. Mary's Roman Catholic Cathedral who climbed the burning spire of his church to beat out the flames. Survivors remembered that they had taken heart from what appeared to be a huge cross above the burning city formed by mighty pillars of smoke converging from several different directions.

Amid the almost universal devastation, isolated buildings survived the holocaust. The Mint was one, with fifty men to defend it against the advancing fires. It was lucky to have its own water supply, a system installed only ten days before. They managed to save the building, reputedly holding $200 million in gold and bullion.

Help came from many quarters. The National Guard was called out by the Governor of California, their numbers augmented by six hundred cadets from the University of California cadet force. Inter-city rivalry was forgotten in the need of the moment when desperate messages went out to Los Angeles for bread and cooked food. Among the earliest to perish were the ornamental ducks on Lake Merced, and roast duck featured on many a menu. Exorbitant food prices were asked, until profiteering of all sorts was brought under control.

People camped in any open space.          Park across the Bay.
Well-dressed refugees in Oakland          Illustrated London News

A little Disfigured, but still in the Ring
MEN WANTED.

The San Francisco spirit. A typical example of the courage, fortitude and refusal to be beaten that makes the aftermath of the San Francisco earthquake one of the shining examples of the triumph of a community in face of disaster.

Illustrated London News

Amid the confusion, families became separated, and the hunt by parents for their children, and by children for anyone they knew, began. Anxiety was expressed by survivors who wanted to reassure relatives in other parts of America or elsewhere. Western Union, whose communications were mainly severed and the rest heavily overloaded by essential traffic, sent five thousand messages by train. More intimate notes fluttered on hoardings and boards, and newspapers were full of small ads arranging rendezvous, and seeking to contact friends and relatives. The various societies in San Francisco, The Elks, Woodmen of the Wild, The Oddfellows and others, showed the real value of their fraternities in caring for their members and helping reunite their families. Badges sprouted on jackets telling members of this or that fraternity to report to a chosen rendezvous. Lovers, determined never to be separated again, sought to be married without delay. Fortunately one of the clerks had had the presence of mind to bring out a book of blank marriage licences from City Hall before it was destroyed. He had never been so busy; marriages were taking place at a rate of seven per hour.

In the Presidio, Jefferson Square, Golden Gate Park and other open places in the city, people congregated seeking protection. Even here they were not wholly safe. Cinders and burning embers fell throughout the day and night, requiring constant vigilance to prevent clothes or belongings being set on fire. "It was a weird twilight," described one survivor, "The glare from the burning city threw a kind of red flame and shadow about us. It seemed uncanny; the figures around us moved like ghosts. The wind and fog blew chill from the ocean, and we walked about to keep warm."

Tent cities sprang up. Aid poured in from across the States and from abroad. In time, these makeshift towns were replaced by more substantial relief camps, but the first tents were adequate and the small communities were organized and fed. Evacuation was a prime concern. During the early days of the fire, terrified people gathered near the ferry station which led to safety in Oakland and Berkeley across the bay. As each ferry arrived, they swept through the gates, threatening to swamp the boats; anyone that fell in the rush was doomed. Later, the procession became more orderly, and it was estimated that between fifty and seventy thousand people found sanctuary across the water. The South Pacific Railway brought in trainloads of supplies and stores of all kinds, free of charge, and took out any whose homes were in other states. William Randolph Hearst, born a San Franciscan and owner of the *San Francisco Examiner*, organised a major relief program for the stricken city, and through his power and influence helped force a massive $4.5 million aid bill through Congress.

San Francisco gradually started to come to life again. Eight days after the disaster, the papers announced with pride that the street cars were running, electricity was to be resumed in three districts that very night, and forty telephones were operating. The long painful process of rebuilding had begun. The casualty figures were never known for sure, but there were estimates of 700 deaths, and 28,000 houses destroyed in America's greatest natural disaster. Lawrence Harris wrote:

> Put me somewhere west of East Street where there's nothing left but dust,
> Where the lads are all abustlin' and where everything's gone bust,
> Where the buildings that are standing sort of blink and blindly stare
> At the damnest finest ruins ever gazed on anywhere.

Two years later, in 1908, a catastrophic earthquake struck the Sicilian town of Messina. The town was not unused to disasters. It had been subject to countless earthquakes and tremors over the ages, and several of a large magnitude, such as the one in 1783 which had killed 30,000 people. Earthquakes were not the only scourge of Messina. In 1740 a plague had ravaged the city; in 1848 the place had been bombarded from the sea; six years later a cholera epidemic had wiped out 16,000 people.

Forgetting the ravages that had gone before, the city had risen again and again. The magnificent natural harbor was far too well situated to be abandoned, and so, the city was persistently rebuilt over and over and knocked down each time.

Messina was a place of beauty. Its fine, sickle-shaped harbor and port, the eighth largest in Italy, was a haven from the easterly gales which howled across the Mediterranean. The town was largely built on the alluvial sands bordering the confluence of five streams which descended from the distant heights to the west, and the whole area was seismically active – engineers

The Straits of Messina during an
earthquake. A contemporary print.

British Museum

were often complaining that the submarine cables laid to the mainland were
being snapped by wayward movements of the ocean floor. It was the subsoil
which was to be responsible for the great damage resulting from the earthquake of 1908. After the 1783 calamity an observer had written, "a larger
part of the misfortune of Messina can be attributed to the lack of solidity in
the structure of the buildings." What was true then was still largely true 125
years later. Behind the port, in the main part of the town, were broad streets
and fine white palazzos, and when the quake came, they could have been
made of icing sugar.

Just before dawn on the Monday morning after Christmas, 1908, as many
were sleeping off the merrymaking of the previous days, the earthquake
struck. Afterward they recalled that there had been warnings of what was
to come. Some previous shocks, including a particularly severe one on
December 5, had shaken the surrounding district. The day before the great
quake too, people later remembered that they had seen a thin cloud of glowing
vapor over the sea and the peasants said somberly that the death fires had
danced that night on the hills across the Strait of Messina.

For thirty-five seconds the earth vibrated in one prolonged tremor, whose
epicenter was calculated at the north entrance to the Straits of Messina
separating Sicily from the mainland of Italy. The terrified inhabitants woke
to the noise of collapsing buildings, towers and chimneys, and the screams
of the injured. One man felt himself lifted in the air, swung backward and
forward for some seconds, then being let down by jerks and jars. Another,

The waterfront after the earthquake and tsunami of 1908. Little but the facades of the once-fine houses remain.

Illustrated London News

The swift arrival of foreign warships saved Messina from total anarchy. Here are Russian sailors bringing out the injured from the ruins after the earthquake in 1908.

Illustrated London News

who had been in the street at the time of the quake, said that at first he had heard a low whistling sound which grew nearer and nearer until it broke into the most terrifying noise he had ever heard in his life, a noise which seemed to be all around him, and to go on and on.

It was pitch dark and raining. At the first tremor the gas main had fractured, so the city was plunged into darkness. Into this darkness, the terrified people of Messina fled, stark naked, and not knowing which way to turn. The submarine cable had snapped at the initial shock and first news of the great disaster was brought to the mainland by an Italian torpedo boat, but it was not until nightfall that Rome heard of the dreadful calamity.

In a nearby town, the author Alexander Hood was sleeping. He was woken by "shouts, wailings, imprecations, desperate cries of terror and of appeal to the saints, accompanied by the barking of dogs. The night suddenly became one of indescribable uproar. The clamor continued as shock succeeded shock." As the day wore on and the earth stilled, dreadful rumors started to spread. At first they were whispered in doubt, and then with greater urgency: "*Messina non e piu!* (Messina no more) *Messina non e piu!*" It seemed inconceivable that the great city had been wholly obliterated. When the first authentic reports began to come in, it was true – *Messina non e piu!*

The first shock had done most damage, and succeeding ones made sure of Messina's fate. But another hazard lay in store for the stricken city. On board a British ship in port was a young sailor, and he wrote, "All hands being asleep when the first shock came and was quickly followed by another – we were all soon on deck and making for the bridge. The darkness was so dense that we could not see what was the matter; and the dust and sulphur that filled the air was choking everyone. We could hardly get our breath. The cries from the shore were something awful. We had all managed to scramble on to the bridge when the Captain gave orders to swing out the port boats when the ship commenced to fall over on her starboard side and we all thought we were turning over. . . . I cannot explain what was the cause of our going over, unless it was the tidal wave causing our bilge plates to catch on the quay, for with the return of the wave we righted again. The cries from the shore then suddenly ceased so I expect the people who had lined the quayside had been washed away as all the boats in the harbor were carried out by the wave."

A tsunami had succeeded the earthquake. It was not a large one, but it was enough to sweep out into the straits many people who had sought safety along the harbor. Alex Munthe, the author, recalled that a huge shark was later washed up on shore, and set upon by the starving people who were horrified to find inside the leg of a woman wearing a red stocking, doubtless one of the victims of the tsunami. The wave, never more than 18 feet (5.4 m) high at Messina reached 16 feet (4.8 m) at Reggio across the Straits and destroyed the wharf. Taormina, Catania and Syracuse were also all affected, and just under two hours from striking Messina, the wave, by then a dwarf little more than three feet high (0.9 m) reached Malta.

There was no fire. The houses were mainly built of stone, and although fractured gas mains caught fire in a number of places and some buildings were razed to the ground, the steady rain quenched any greater outbreak.

Even without the added hazard of fire, Messina had taken more than enough punishment. Fifty miles (80.5 km) on either side of the straits of Messina, villages had been flattened, towns ruined and people killed. But their agony was nothing to that of Messina itself. At first sight in Messina, and in Reggio across the water, streets gave the impression of being hardly damaged. Facades were standing, but behind the facades was . . . nothing. Each and every house had dissolved into a pile of rubble. The loss of life was appalling. The correct total was never discovered because so many documents were lost, but it was believed that the death toll in Messina alone was 100,000, and in Reggio 20,000, while in smaller towns and villages it was calculated that a further 30,000 more had lost their lives.

As soon as he could get there, Alexander Hood rode to Messina. "The long line of stately palaces which looked upon the harbour and lilac mountains of Calabria were now mounds of limedust and broken stone, of beams and broken tiles. Facades stood as if mocking – hiding nothing. There was nothing left of the city behind." The quay had sunk several feet and the tsunami had left nothing but fruit and broken barrels. The Duomo, the cathedral, was in ruins. Its monolithic granite pillars with gilded capitals were still standing. On the floor of the nave were the remains of the great roof. Only the dome of the apse at the east end had survived, with its colossal mosaic figure of Christ blessing the ruins of Messina.

The earthquake had destroyed the army barracks, entombing the garrison of 800 soldiers. Only 14 were rescued alive. When the railway station collapsed, 40 railwaymen lost their lives. Only seven survived of the Messina police force. The jail, which housed some of Sicily's worst criminals, collapsed like a house of cards, freeing 650 men and women who immediately set about ransacking the ruined houses and robbing the dead and injured. When an Italian torpedo boat landed that afternoon the crew were forced to retreat by a gang who were engaged in blowing open the vaults of the Bank of Italy trying to get at the huge quantity of money inside.

News was late getting to Rome, and positive action by the Italian government was later still, but there were others nearer at hand. The fleets of several European navies were cruising in the area. First on the scene was a Russian squadron. A few hours later five ships of the British navy, which had steamed from Malta, had anchored and were ready to give assistance. Six hundred Russian seamen, and as many British sailors, went ashore to restore order, feed the hungry and help the injured. The two fleets stayed there for a week and the assistance they rendered was priceless. Without it the town would have dissolved into anarchy. It was an impressive demonstration of international aid.

Martial law was declared, but not for several days was order restored. The resident thieves were joined by brigands from the hills and peasants from the villages around who were carried away by the sight of unguarded riches and valuable possessions.

One of the first contingents of troops was a party of Sicilian born cavalry-men. As the steamer approached the devastated city, a correspondent watched the agonized men looking on their ruined city and wrote: "The Sicilian troopers on board used their borrowed glasses and, bit by bit, picked out details of the ruins, still smoking gently here and there. They recognised where this or that church, or college had stood, and gave low cries of pain. There was no loud moaning; here and there some drab little old man was querulous and complaining. Could he not get ashore? His house, he feared, was gone with those in it. He wished to know. 'Patience', said the officer at the gangway. But all were patient, incredibly patient. As the ferry neared shore it was besieged by small boats. Anxiously those on board sought information. Questions poured down on the boatmen: 'My father, is he alive?' 'And my wife?' 'And mine?' . . . It was all wonderfully quiet, and I did not hear one sound of loud wailing. The querulous old men whined pitifully, begging to be allowed ashore, and two or three women lay back in deckchairs worn out and crying silently – that was all."

By January 4 it seemed that no one could be alive. Already the smell of putrifying corpses, human and animal, was giving the authorities grave concern. The risk of disease was high. Yet, here and there, people were still being rescued alive. On January 6, nine days after the quake, ten more were found buried, bringing the total rescued from the ruins to 2,300. The same day the captain of the fort was found alive, entombed in a cellar beneath his house. The general in command wanted to evacuate and seal off the city, use dynamite to bring down the remaining ruins and let the plague, if it came, to run its course away from the population. On January 7, the Archbishop stood on top of the highest roof still standing and blessed the dead. Messina was sealed off and made a proscribed area. On January 12, some people were discovered alive and well in a cellar, where they had lived off oil and vege-tables. On January 15, eighteen days after the disaster had struck, more people were rescued alive. Then the decision to dynamite or not to dynamite was taken out of the hands of the authorities and nature took a hand. A heavy tremor struck the remains of the city. When the pall of dust had cleared, nothing remained standing. If people were alive in cellars or under-ground rooms then they were doomed, for the city collapsed on top of them.

The city was abandoned, and the troops in charge could go about the grisly task of razing the remains. Corpses were put in huge graves, covered in quicklime and the graves filled in. More quicklime was scattered over Messina, while officials set about looking for priceless art and ecclesiastical treasures which were known to be buried. Most were recovered intact. Others set about digging towards the vaults of the banks, and before the last tremor, the vaults were discovered unopened, their contents untouched by fire.

International assistance was immediate and open-handed. Money and aid poured in. The United States Congress appropriated $800,000 for the victims of the earthquake in addition to the $1 million raised by the American Red Cross. Other contributions were as generous and unsparing. Three thousand wooden-framed houses were shipped across the Atlantic to provide shelter for the destitute. The Swiss, German and other governments founded orphanages for the parentless children of Messina and Calabria. It was an impressive show of international aid: immediate aid for rescue and assistance, and long-term aid for the rehabilitation of the survivors. A pattern which has been repeated on countless occasions was just beginning.

The Italian government decided not to rebuild Messina, but in 1912, four years after the great disaster, the decision was reversed because the site was too valuable and the harbor indispensable. The ruins were leveled and consolidated with concrete, then everything was covered with a thin layer of loose sand. Buildings were limited to two stories with reinforced concrete and frames, and the streets were built wide enough so that if the houses fell outward during any future quake, the thoroughfares would not be blocked. At first the regulations were strictly adhered to, but as time passed higher buildings have appeared on the periphery of the city. Messina survived

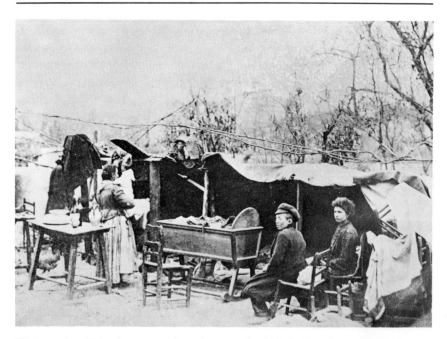

The people of Messina camped out in the streets under any form of makeshift shelter they could find, and shivered in the cold.

Allied bombing in the war and withstood the effects of several lesser earthquakes, but there has not yet been another earthquake like the one which led to the great disaster of 1908.

The importance of immediate outside aid was shown in the great Japanese disaster of 1923. It was lucky that Yokohama was a great international port. At anchor the day of the earthquake, apart from the *Empress of Australia*, was the *Korea Maru* and many smaller ships. One of the latter was the little steamer *Dongola*, and her captain later wrote to the owners: "The ship commenced to tremble and vibrate violently and on looking towards the shore it was seen that a terrible earthquake was taking place, buildings were collapsing in all directions and in a few minutes nothing could be seen for clouds of dust."

The piers and wharves were burning fiercely. The quay where relatives and friends were seeing off the passengers on board the *Empress of Australia* sunk almost immediately at both ends leaving those on it stranded as if they had been on an island. All along the waterfront boats cast off their lines and sought open water. It was a difficult progress, menaced by ships of all sizes and nationalities. The *Dongola* was touched by one ship, but no damage was caused. There were drifting and burning lighters and barges. One of these, the *Dongola's* captain reported, struck his ship and sank throwing the occupants into the water; some were rescued but others drowned. The *Dongola* sailed that evening for the port of Kobe bearing 550 survivors – two of whom died on the way and were buried at sea.

Police Superintendant Morioka became the hero of Yokohama. With all communications destroyed he tried every means he knew to tell the world of the great city's plight. From the radio cabin of the *Korea Maru* Superintendent Morioka managed to transmit his vital message. It was picked up by the American Asiatic Squadron then cruising off southern China, and they immediately made full steam for the stricken port. The signal was picked up by others and transmitted so that the world knew of the terrible disaster that had struck Japan's greatest port. But did Tokyo know?

There was no way of knowing except by sending a messenger. At three o'clock in the morning, fifteen hours after the first tremor, two police inspectors came aboard the *Korea Maru* seeking their chief. They were ordered to make their way immediately to Tokyo to report what had happened. They set off on foot to cover the thirty miles (48.3 km) of ruined and battered city and country. The following afternoon, after no rest and no food and after being on duty continuously for twenty-four hours they reached a blackened and still burning Tokyo. They made their way to the Ministry of War and gave their message. At last those in the government knew the size of the crisis facing Yokohama. With the promise that troops would be sent immediately, the two policemen returned the way they had come, reporting en route to every single police post and military headquarters to say that matters were

Anxiously survivors look for news of relatives on the noticeboards that sprung up across Tokyo after the disastrous fire. Illustrated London News

in order, troops on the way, and to end rumors. Twenty-four hours after leaving Yokohama they once again reported to Morioka and notices were posted to the effect that troops were on the way. Almost as soon as these notices were displayed the first destroyer-load of Japanese troops arrived.

There was little risk of lawlessness. Editor Kinney commented on the stoicism of the people of Yokohama, and their attitude of *shikataganai* (it can't be helped) in face of unparalleled disaster. In Kinney's opinion, this fatalism sometimes had a bad effect, because many fires might have been stopped had those nearby shown any initiative and put them out. Instead, people watched the sparks gather strength, ignite each house in turn, and then start to burn until no one without proper fire fighting equipment could have hoped to stop the gathering inferno.

Just as the people of Lisbon 168 years before would have turned on heretics as the cause of their misfortune, it was the Koreans that the Japanese blamed. Seizing on any excuse or supposed provocation, the Japanese killed any Korean, or suspected Korean. It is doubtful whether Koreans or anyone else had a deliberate hand in the destruction of Tokyo and Yokohama, but to crazed minds, anything was possible. The arrival of soldiers nipped such disturbances in the bud, and the task of rebuilding Tokyo and Yokohama began in earnest when the fires had died and the embers cooled.

The tragic hunt for anything left of
their homes begins amid the incredible
devastation to Japan's capital city.
Radio Times Hulton Picture Library

The importance of reimposing law and order after a disaster was shown at
Port Royal after the quake of 1692. The rector of the church was perhaps
the most lucid survivor of the great earthquake. He wrote later: "The Day
when all this befel us was very clear, and afforded not the Suspicion of the
least Evil; but in the Space of three Minutes, about half an Hour after eleven
in the Morning, Port-Royal, the fairest Town of all the English Plantations,
the best Emporium and Mart of this Part of the World, exceeding in its
Riches, plentiful of all good Things, was shaken and shattered to Pieces,
sunk-into and covered, for the greater Part, by the Sea, and will in a short
Time be wholly eaten-up by it. . . ."

On Wednesday, June 7, the rector had been at his church reading prayers,
a practice which he had maintained since his arrival in order to keep up some
"Shew of Religion among a most ungodly debauched People," as he described his flock. The rector continued, "I was gone to a Place hard by the
Church, where the Merchants used to meet, and where the President of the
Council was. This Gentleman came into my Company, and engaged me to
take a Glass of Wormwood Wine with him, as a Whet before Dinner."

"No sooner started that I found the Ground Rowling and moving under
my Feet, upon which I said, 'Lord, Sir, what's this?' He replied very com-
posedly, being a very grave man, 'It is an earthquake, be not afraid, it will
soon be over.' "

The rector made toward the solid fort and "saw the Earth open and
swallow-up a Multitude of People, and the Sea mounting-in upon us over

Italian soldiers ready for duty after
the Messina earthquake of 1908.

Radio Times Hulton Picture Library

US sailors guarding a store wrecked       earthquake of 1933.
in the Long Beach, California

Southern California Earthquake Pictures

the Fortifications. . . . When I came into the Streets every one laid hold on my Cloaths and embraced me, that with their Fear and Kindness I was almost stifled. I persuaded them at last to kneel down and make a large Ring, which they did, I prayed with them near an Hour, when I was almost spent with the Heat of the Sun, and the Exercise. They then brought me a Chair; the Earth working all the while with new Motions, and Tremblings, like the Rowlings of the Sea. As soon as Night came on, a Company of lewd Rogues, whom they call Privateers, fell to breaking open Ware-houses, and Houses deserted, to rob and rifle their Neighbours whilst the Earth trembled under them and the Houses fell on some of them in the Act; and those audacious Whores who remain still upon the Place, are as impudent and drunken as ever."

While Port Royal was given over to the "lewd rogues," the rector remained on board a ship in the harbor. "Ever since that fatal day," he wrote, "the most terrible that I ever had in my life, I have lived on board a Ship, for the shaking of the Earth returns every now and then. Yesterday we had a very great one, but it seems less terrible on shipboard than on Shore. Yet I have returned to Port Royal three Times among the shattered Houses to be visited, to bury the Dead, pray with the Sick and chasten the Children. The people are overjoyed to see me among them and wept as I preached. I hope by this terrible Judgement God will make them reform their Lives for there is not a more Ungodly People on the Face of the Earth."

The condition of those at Port Royal was common to most earthquake victims. The immediate effect was one of stupefaction, almost of mental paralysis. They were stunned. As an observer quickly on the scene after a more modern earthquake said, tears were seldom seen, it was as a witness of the Lisbon quake had described, "beyond tears." People told of their experiences with apparent unconcern as though they had been disinterested spectators. They went about their work, numbed. The rescued had no idea of the passage of time. Some thought they had been buried a matter of hours, not days. Kinney wrote immediately after the great Tokyo earthquake "Already the disaster seemed strangely old, as if one had lived in the atmosphere of misery for years; as if normal times, orderly routine of business and three meals a day were a thing remote, a long past period of peace." A state of total bewilderment is common in disasters, and not only earthquakes, and was vividly described by a survivor of the Lisbon catastrophe, "An Embrace and Tears could only express the Commotion of our Minds. . . ."

There had been no warning in Lisbon, but those in Agadir, Morocco on Monday February 29, 1960 might have noticed strange events during the morning and afternoon. The many animals in the town seemed strangely restless. Donkeys and horses stirred in the stables, struggled against their tethers and kicked against their stable walls. Dogs howled for no apparent reason, and cats behaved oddly. People found that they had to keep adjusting ctures on their walls, and later it was heard that a small boy had been soundly scolded for allowing a bucket to spill over, yet he had sworn that he never touched it. Some went to bed early that night, only to be awakened by strange knockings on their doors. An English couple sitting in a cinema, suddenly and for no reason that they could explain afterward, decided to get up and leave. They walked toward the beach, and as they did, the earthquake struck.

Two faults pass under Agadir, part of the great Atlas fault that stretches across North Africa, and has caused a number of earthquakes throughout history, some of them very severe. These faults stirred at 11:40 that evening. The movement was not protracted, and it was later estimated to have lasted only eight to ten seconds, but the shift of four feet (1.2 m) horizontally, and four feet vertically was immense, and enough to shatter the most solid foundations and constructions. The buildings at Agadir were not very soundly built, and the tremor was enough to raze Agadir to the ground, "as completely as the Romans once obliterated Carthage," as one observer later reported. A pilot flying over the ruined town said it looked as though "a giant foot has stepped on it and squashed it flat." 70 percent of Agadir was demolished.

In those incredible ten seconds, twelve thousand people were estimated to have died. Many of these were in mosques, as it was the height of Ramadan. Ancient buildings stood up no better that the modern constructions in the

Not even modern reinforced concrete buildings could withstand the incredible ground movement during the Agadir earthquake of 1960.

Professor N.N. Ambraseys

city, which was beginning to gather a reputation as a tourist resort. The quake severed all power lines, and the place was plunged into darkness. In this darkness, the first rescue operations were carried out.

With the dawn, it was possible to see the total devastation that was now Agadir, and the immensity of the problem facing the rescuers was only too apparent. In heat which at times reached 105°F (40.6°C) the need for speed was paramount, but within a day the putrid stench of rotting bodies under the ruins and rubble was all-pervading. Despite these appalling conditions, and the added risk of rabid dogs and rats, the rescuers worked away without rest.

Moroccan troops were quickly on the scene; a French naval squadron led by the aircraft carrier *Lafayette* was ordered to sail to Agadir to assist with all speed; sailors from the US Sixth Fleet dug at first with hope, then with increasing despair in the ruins. King Mohammed V of Morocco pledged his personal fortune as surety for the rebuilding of Agadir, and Prince Hassan, the present king, was personally in charge of rescue operations.

The International Red Cross mounted an immense aid and rehabilitation program, and assistance for Agadir poured in from across the globe. There were many lessons learned in the relief operation at Agadir. No one realized that within three years international aid was going to be needed, and on an even greater scale.

The clock on the railway station stopped at 5:17 A.M. on the morning of July 26, 1963 at Skopje in the valley of the Vardar in Macedonia, Yugoslavia. There had been no warning of the earthquake except a rumble in the earth which in seconds had become a soul-shattering roar. The noise of the quake died and was succeeded by the equally terrible noise of falling buildings and collapsing roofs, walls and chimneys.

Skopje was no stranger to disaster. Two previous earthquakes had completely destroyed the city, in 518 and 1555, but this latest catastrophe with a magnitude of 6.0 on the Richter scale exceeded anything known in Europe since the earthquake at Messina in 1908. Most people were in bed and asleep when the quake struck, and most of the 1,070 dead were killed where they slept. But many more were buried under the mountains of rubble where 16,000 homes had been utterly destroyed and a further 28,000 damaged to some degree. Within hours the biggest international relief program ever mounted was underway. And all the aid possible was needed.

The devastation in parts of Skopje was complete, and in a number of smaller towns and villages around. All that remained of some apartment buildings constructed since the war was an anonymous pile of broken concrete and twisted steel. But in the ruins lay people, some dead, some alive but injured, some still alive but trapped. Luckily, although their barracks collapsed like a child's toy under a heavy foot, the military garrison of

The clock on the railway station at Skopje in Yugoslavia stopped at 5:17 that summer morning of July 26, 1963.

Skopje

Skopje were outside. They were the first rescuers to arrive. In the first hours, thanks to the efforts of the soldiers and the people of Skopje six thousand people were rescued, but a further ten thousand still lay buried.

By nine o'clock in the morning a complete field hospital had been set up by the Yugoslav army and already streams of medical helpers were on their way to the stricken city. Homes, schools and hostels across the country opened their doors to refugees, many of them children, who came in increasing numbers. Doctors, rescue workers, miners to help dig out victims in the ruins, and people of many nations who happened to be in Yugoslavia, and felt that they could help poured into Skopje. Other tourists who had been in Skopje during the earthquake returned home having given their blood to the transfusion units. Many left all their money to the growing relief funds.

Over the city hung a great white cloud of dust. Beneath this pall the

The Citadel. Before and after the
earthquake of July 26, 1963 at Skopje.

Skopje

rescuers worked – a team which in the end numbered over ten thousand people of many nationalities – in slave conditions of sun, heat and the sickly smell of putrifying bodies. The rescuers dug, mainly in perfect silence in case somewhere a faint tapping, or the voice of a trapped person could be heard. The families of those buried waited at one side, sitting on what they had rescued, staring into space. From time to time, and the occasions grew fewer as the days passed, some slight sound might be heard within some seemingly endless pile of rubble and then the efforts became feverish. All were sustained by the thought that perhaps, somewhere there might still be someone still alive. When such a miracle did occur it sustained those who had been at work for hours and days on end. There were some very remarkable tales. One man was found alive and well after being buried for three days, another, the last, was found alive after an incredible eighty hours pinned beneath a small mountain of rubble.

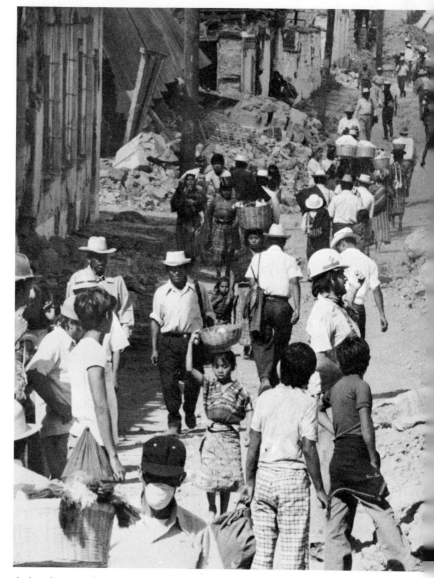

Red Cross help after the Guatemala earthquake of February 1976. One of the fifteen major earthquakes that took place that year.

---

The disaster at Skopje touched the compassion of the world. The United Nations passed a resolution declaring that Skopje would be rebuilt as a gesture of international solidarity. By then doctors and medical teams, equipment and supplies of all sorts had started to come into Skopje in ever increasing numbers. On the first day of the earthquake forty aircraft from many nations had landed at Belgrade and at Skopje itself bringing vitally needed supplies. It was the start of an immense relief and rehabilitation program; on the part of the Macedonian Government, the Federal Government of Yugoslavia, UNESCO, and UNO.

1976 was a year which saw fifteen major earthquakes with magnitudes of over 7.0, and each posed particular problems for international relief organizations. They were not called in for the biggest of all, the great Chinese Tangshan earthquake where some think the death toll was between half and three-quarters of a *million* people. On February 4 at three o'clock in the morning, a 7.5 magnitude quake struck Guatemala. Two days later another quake struck the same area, resulting in a death toll of 22,000 with 77,000 injured and over 1,000,000 people homeless – a fifth of the entire population of the republic. In June and July of that year a succession of earthquakes struck

In the end the efforts of the survivors bring order to chaos and a return to normal living. Street markets were soon doing a flourishing trade after the Guatamala earthquake of 1976.

League of Red Cross Societies

"Nothing left but our eyes to cry with." The pitiful condition and scene of utter devastation following an earthquake. League of Red Cross Societies

Indonesia. One was in the remote province of Irian Jaya at the eastern end of the country, where the population is sparse, but the other occurred on Bali where a belt of damage thirty miles (48.3 km) wide was created in an area where 500,000 people lived, mainly in houses which proved totally vulnerable. Fortunately the death toll was no more than 573, but a further 1,000 were injured and an estimated 250,000 made homeless. In November that year it was the turn of Turkey, and stirrings on the great Anatolian fault caused the destruction of the town of Van in a 7.6 magnitude quake which killed 3,800 people, injured nearly 5,000 more and made 50,000 homeless in the middle of winter. These were just four of the major quakes which occurred that year, and it gives some idea of the massive effort needed in disaster relief – and these were only earthquake disasters. Other natural or man-made disasters also kill, maim or render homeless those in villages, towns and cities. Such events occur every week, in some part of the world.

The efforts of many relief organizations are directed to helping the victims of these disasters – there are said to be four hundred in the United States alone. To try and untangle what was fast becoming a relief muddle, UNDRO (United Nations Disaster Relief Co-Ordinator) was established in 1972. Its role is to mobilize relief quickly, to coordinate the effort of the many agencies, to prevent, or at least minimize, duplication and waste, and to generate contingency planning. At the same time UNDRO does not attempt to supersede the national or representative effort of international organizations, such as those of the League of Red Cross Societies (a world federation of National Red Cross, Red Crescent and Red Lion and Sun Societies).

The vast and complex world of relief – immediate, and long term rehabilitation – is outside the scope of this book, but however much may still be needed in the way of coordination and assessing the real needs after a disaster, things have gone a long way since shiploads of shovels and pickaxes were sent to the stricken city of Lisbon.

# 6
# Survival in
# an Earthquake

THE DAMAGE CAUSED by an earthquake can be measured in more than human lives, although it is this tragic aspect that usually hits the headlines. Often those who survive feel that they are worse off than those who perished. The loss of health, family, relatives, and friends – the entire framework of life – can have a devastating effect on a person's future. To a nation, the economic, social, and other implications can be just as profound.

The $240 million damage resulting from the Alaskan earthquake of 1964 was soon absorbed in the vast economy of the United States. But the losses which followed the 1963 earthquake in Skopje, Yugoslavia – one that was three thousand times less violent – amounted to $1,000 million, a sum nearly equivalent to the entire annual budget of that country. The earthquake which hit Guatemala in 1976 killed 25,000, injured 77,000, and made nearly a quarter of the population of the country homeless. These are figures to conjure with.

Recently, the only major earthquakes to strike densely populated areas have been those at Bucharest in March 1977, and Salonika in June 1978. Here the casualties would have been much higher, if it had not been a hot night with many people sleeping outdoors. Tokyo was shaken by the Migayi earthquake off northern Honshu eight days before the Salonika quake. Bland official figures announced in the Japanese capital a few days earlier had stated that in the event of a repeat of the Kanto earthquake of 1923, casualties of no less than 36,000 could be expected.

Earthquake emergency planning is now receiving urgent consideration in many countries. Planning for community education, for the setting up of national disaster relief agencies, and for the coordination of resources in the event of an emergency is being undertaken. These contingency arrangements are the responsibility of governments, national and regional, and of more local authorities. The ordinary person can do little except exert every pressure to ensure that such plans exist and are kept up-to-date.

But in every earthquake, as in every other disaster, in the end the authorities must rely on the good sense, and where possible the disaster training of ordinary citizens, for it is they and they alone who are in the best position

This broken telephone pole and festoon of wires frames the devastation in Hilo, Hawaii, after the tsunami of 1960 had passed.

International Tsunami Information Center

to save their own lives. On many occasions San Francisco has been held up as the shining example of how a community should behave in a disaster. But this example was more than a resurgence of the old pioneering spirit, with its unconscious heroism, unselfishness and ebullience. Beneath it lay the day to day commonsense and civilized attitude of ordinary people. In particular, they cooperated with the troops sent in to help bring the city back to normality. The danger of an epidemic breaking out was tremendous with the escape of thousands of rats, the fracturing of sewers, and the lack of any drainage. Proclamations and instructions told San Franciscans what they should or should not do, but the fact that disease was prevented was largely due to the good sense and careful hygiene of the citizens rather than to any proclamation. All this took place without any disaster training or education, or any training in self-help.

We know better now. There is a great deal that the ordinary citizen can do to help themselves and those around them in an earthquake.

We cannot prevent an earthquake. On many occasions we will not be forewarned that it is going to occur and it will come as a complete and horrifying surprise. But there are a number of commonsense precautions which everyone who lives in an earthquake-prone area should take in their own interest, and in those of their family and community. There is inevitably great danger in an earthquake, but there are ways to minimize it and knowledge lessens panic. These precautions can be divided into what should be done before, during and after an earthquake.

# BEFORE

There are a number of safeguards that every household should take. The first of these is to have somewhere to keep emergency equipment. It could be a cupboard or closet, a box or a case or even a drawer, but wherever you choose it must be accessible, in hall or passage rather than in attic or cellar.

In this safety cache should be a flashlight, with spare batteries – as an earthquake might strike at night and all electricity be cut off. There should also be a battery-powered radio, not one for general use in the family but one which is kept permanently for emergency purposes. This is perhaps the single most useful piece of equipment as there is every likelihood of telephone lines coming down in a severe tremor. In any case telephone switchboards will be jammed with emergency calls. The authorities will make any announcements they have by radio – it is probable that electricity failure will make television sets useless. For those living in tsunami-prone areas, a radio is their lifeline. Further, everyone must be in touch with what is going on. By doing so you will ease the considerable problems of many sorts which fall to local authorities who must organize and coordinate rescue and relief in a disaster.

A first-aid kit is another essential item to have in an emergency cache. A reserve of food and water is also advisable. Water should be in plastic bottles, food is best kept in an immediately consumable form, in cans for instance. This too is for emergency use only.

These are the essential contents of the emergency store, but if space allows other items might well be included. Blankets might be very useful should it be necessary to evacuate the house in cold weather or at night. Other warm clothes such as spare sweaters, parkas or gloves would also be of great value in an emergency.

One thing the store should never contain are matches, as a naked light would be fatal should a gas main fracture. Under no circumstances should a naked light be used until a thorough inspection has been made after an earthquake to ensure that there is no gas leak. This applies to turning on any electrical switch as this will create a spark.

The risk of pipes and mains fracturing due to ground movement in an earthquake is very great. Sometimes, too, the effect of such ground movement is difficult to detect. A complete inspection should be made after an earthquake to ensure that all is as it should be. It may be necessary or advisable to turn off electricity, water or gas, and every responsible member of

The aftermath of an earthquake. This entire family was killed in Skopje, Yugoslavia on July 26, 1963.

League of Red Cross Societies

---

the household should know where the main switches or valves are located.

Knowledge of elementary first aid is an essential ingredient of any household disaster planning (most civic authorities or the local Red Cross or ambulance services run first aid courses). Such knowledge might save life or suffering, but it is certain to save the valuable time of those medical personnel needed to deal with the more seriously injured.

It is sensible to have earthquake disaster practice to ensure that everyone, particularly children, understand what they must do in the event of an earthquake. It has been found on many occasions that such knowledge and earthquake education lessens panic and gives confidence. Individual self-help really does minimize death and injury.

Within every house there are many potentially lethal objects: heavy pieces of furniture or kitchen equipment that are not properly secured to walls; heavy objects on high shelves which might be dislodged in a severe tremor; and many others. It is necessary to make a minute inspection of the house to ensure that the risk of death, damage or injury through sheer carelessness is reduced to the minimum.

Water heaters, refrigerators, cookers, washing machines, and other heavy appliances which might move during a tremor, should be bolted to the floor or firmly secured to the wall. In case this should fail, it is sensible to have them connected to water, gas or electricity mains by long flexible connections. Rigid pipes, short flexes or other connections fracture easily when appliances break free. Heavy pieces of furniture or other heavy but movable objects should be secured to prevent them crossing the floor and crushing anything in their path, or even plunging through a far wall. Shelves, bookcases or storage cabinets are also potential death dealers, especially if heavy

The search for survivors. A seemingly impossible task in an Iranian village after the earthquake of 1968. The timberless adobe-type construction of these dwellings with immensely thick and heavy roofs proved totally vulnerable in an earthquake shock of even moderate intensity.

Professor N.N. Ambraseys

books or objects are placed on the upper shelves. The whole bookcase or cabinet should be secured to the wall; heavier objects confined to the lower shelves, and in extreme cases even secured to the shelves they are resting on.

Outside, it will be difficult to carry out a proper inspection for earthquake risk without professional guidance. Therefore it is necessary to call in a competent engineer trained to recognize and deal with earthquake engineering hazards. It is possible that reinforcing might be necessary, but only an expert eye might recognize that this is so. If purchasing a house in an earthquake zone, it is essential to call on expert advice before buying, not only to find out the essential reliability of the structure itself, but also to discover details of the siting and subsoil and to be informed of the seismic risk and geological peculiarities of the district chosen. Having carried this out, ensure that earthquake insurance is up to date and provides adequate cover, bearing in mind rising prices and the cost of replacing or rebuilding in your district.

Even in the best-ordered communities there is always a risk of disease or epidemic after a disaster such as an earthquake, especially if sewers are fractured, or poor hygiene should follow an earthquake or exist in relief camps. Ensure the family's immunization is kept fully up-to-date.

Finally, there is a growing awareness in earthquake countries of the great risks that their populations run. Some hazard reduction measures can be conducted at government or state level, but much can only be dealt with by local authorities. It is the duty of every one to support and reinforce every measure that might minimize earthquake damage, help enforce local safe building codes – especially for such buildings as schools and hospitals – earthquake precautions, earthquake education – for both adults and schools – or any other actions that might make your community a safer, more efficient place to live.

# DURING

During the quake itself the primary consideration is to remain calm and not to panic. Panic may not only put your own life at risk, it might also endanger the lives of others, for panic has been shown on innumerable occasions to be the most contagious of diseases.

If indoors during a quake it is usually better to stay there. Few towns have wide enough streets. Houses, walls, tiles and other roof objects may be flung into the street below – in San Francisco someone measured that a brick from the parapet of one building had been catapulted some forty feet (12 m) into the roadway. Balconies, advertising signs, awnings and other ornaments which adorn a great many houses become potentially lethal missiles during an earthquake. And there have been numerous instances of people running into the street only to be crushed by something falling on them from a roof or high wall.

Inside a building it is essential to watch out for falling objects, swinging chandeliers or other light fittings, falling plaster, heavy objects or pieces of furniture careering across a floor, or pictures swinging or tumbling from walls. The safest place in a room is against a wall or in a corner or under the stout lintel of a door frame. Under a bed, strong table or desk may give even greater protection.

Occupants of office blocks face different hazards. Most of these buildings are multistory and equipped with elevators or escalators. Avoid these, as you may well be trapped in them or on them in the event of the electricity failing. Stairways are also potential deathtraps as there may be a general rush for the exits and the danger of crushing becomes greater than from the quake itself. Most modern office blocks are full of glass – great glass windows, glass partitions, glass skylights or mirrors. These are liable not only to break, but to fragment into slivers as lethal as any arrow. So choose a place to shelter away from glass, if that is possible.

Factories pose special problems as the danger here lies in heavy machinery or other installations sliding or moving across the floor. Theaters and stores with limited exits and possibly many loose fittings can be perilous in an earthquake. Once again the importance of not panicking and rushing those exits is paramount. Open sports stadia too pose problems, the safest place here is the middle of the arena or field.

Narrow streets filled with debris. Many who rushed out of their homes during the Messina earthquake of 1908 were crushed to death by falling roofs and masonry.

Radio Times Hulton Picture Library

If outside, it is essential to keep well away from high buildings or masonry walls. Electric or telegraph poles are only too easily dislodged, posing not only a danger of crushing those below, but also of dropping live wires. Thus any wires seen lying on the ground must not be touched under any circumstances. For anyone finding themselves outside in a quake it is best to hurry to a wide open space – and stay there. If driving, also make for an open space and remain there in the car, listening to the radio for any announcements.

If you should happen to become trapped, remember that very soon people will be looking for you. If you panic you may dislodge some object or beam, which could fall and crush you, it is therefore essential to remain still, conserving your strength and listening to the approach of rescuers. Rescue equipment often includes sophisticated listening devices. Tapping on a pipe or beam can be heard for a considerable distance, and this is often a better way of letting people know where you are than shouting which can exhaust you and may not be heard.

## AFTER

Once the tremors have died down the first requirement is to see if those around you are alright. Give first aid where necessary. The more severely injured should be left where they are and not moved – but made comfortable and above all warm – unless there is danger of further injury from falling walls, roofs or ceilings. Medical assistance should be summoned directly.

As soon as possible, check your house for broken gas or water mains, fractured electrical connections and above all, fires. If looking in closet or cupboard, take care that the contents will not fall on your head when you open the doors. Do not use the toilet until it is clear that the sewers are still intact. In the event of the water supply being fractured, emergency water can always be found in the water heater or tank, the lavatory cistern, as melted ice cubes and in the last extremity in cans of fruit and vegetables.

You should concentrate on eating all fresh or perishable food before turning to the canned supply. Cooking should never take place indoors until gas connections have been examined and the chimney inspected from grate to roof for breaks in the lining. It is better, if the weather is suitable, to cook outside on barbeque or open brazier. If your water supply has been exposed to broken glass, dust or rubble, it should be filtered before drinking with a clean cloth or handkerchief. The public supply should not be used until the authorities say that it remains uncontaminated and fit to drink.

There are often aftershocks succeeding an earthquake and these may be as severe or even more severe than the initial tremor. Your house may be standing, apparently intact, but you will not know if the quake has not so weakened it that it might fall next time. So having turned off gas, water and electricity make your way in an orderly, unhurried fashion to the nearest open space.

A survivor salvages usable material from the ruins of Managua, Nicaragua after the earthquake of 1972 which destroyed 36 blocks (half of the city) in less than 30 seconds. International aid was immediately required to set up

Community self-help is invaluable. Trained volunteer organizations can do a great deal in any disaster – and in many parts of the world these organizations have been given specific tasks for which they can plan ahead. On other occasions – such as in the Guatemala earthquake when the Guatemala Flying Club proved of invaluable assistance in assessing damage and flying mercy missions – organizations, clubs and other bodies with particular skills

medical services, distribute food and
water, and to provide temporary
shelter.                                    Bureau of Public Affairs, US Department of State

---

have performed wonders. But every community, however small can also do
a great deal to help itself.

It should be possible for every street to organize their own plans. Arrange
a rendezvous in the nearest open area where everyone should go in the event
of an earthquake. Know how many are in each house so that if anyone is
missing immediate rescue efforts can be put in hand. Know the sources of

Wearing face masks for protection, Red Cross workers and Yugoslavian soldiers continue the search for dead and injured after the Skopje earthquake of 1963.

League of Red Cross Societies

emergency water supplies – swimming pools, ponds and lakes – to help the fire department. In every rescue operation time is wasted through the inevitable lack of detailed local knowledge – it is the people who live in an area who are in the best position to help the authorities, and prevent, as has happened after many disasters, rescuers looking for people who are not there and wasting precious resources which are only too pressingly needed elsewhere.

Self-help. The services rendered by volunteer organizations after the Tokyo earthquake of 1923 proved invaluable. Members of the Young Men's Association of Japan carrying an old lady to safety.

Radio Times Hulton Picture Library

In any community some people are more vulnerable than others. Recent analysis has shown that casualties after an earthquake fall into constant areas. Babies with the mothers near them are much less at risk than those aged four to fourteen who are physically not strong, nor mature enough to understand unnecessary risk. Least at risk are adults from fourteen upward, and then at the upper age bracket the aged and of course the infirm are probably most vulnerable of all. Therefore it is the children and the old people who require most looking after.

Sightseers after any disaster are not only a hazard to the authorities, and often to themselves, but they severely hamper rescue operations by cluttering roads or deflecting scarce rescue facilities. They place themselves at risk from subsequent secondary fire or explosion. If near the sea, sightseers after an earthquake are at special risk from tsunami. Those in hilly districts are in danger from landslips or landslides.

Immediately after an earthquake it is essential to turn on the radio, and leave it on. Remember that volunteer help may well be needed once an assessment has been made of damage and casualties. So above all cooperate with authorities and rescue workers.

Finally: learn from your experience and those of others – it may happen again.

# 7

# Earthquake Engineering

EARLY WOODEN HOUSES of light framework; stone-built houses little more than hovels; simple structures, which appear as though a breath of wind or the mildest tremor would set them tumbling, survive and have survived the most powerful earthquakes. But as man's accommodation has become more sophisticated and the materials used more complex, earthquake damage has become a serious and expensive problem.

Ancient civilizations knew what to do; those who endured earthquakes or lived in "earthquake country" soon learned how to protect themselves, and there may still be lessons to be found in the construction of their simple dwellings – what earthquake engineers quaintly call "vernacular buildings."

Earthquakes sometimes produce surprising results. The mild quakes which frightened Londoners in 1750 caused practically no damage, despite what one observer said, "We know the Nature of the building of London Houses, which sometimes fall of themselves without shaking – not one fell though twice shaken wonderfully." After earthquakes in Lima, Peru, the residents, looking for any sign from God of His disapproval of the Spaniards, were gratified to notice that the walled foundations of several buildings constructed by the Incas stood firm, while the outwardly solid upper levels built by the Spaniards all tumbled to the ground.

\ Ancient Japanese houses consisted of a light framework put together without struts or ties, with all the timbers crossing one another at right angles. These beams and struts were filled inside with bamboo wattle plastered with mud, and the whole construction rested on large square stones dug into earth. When an earthquake struck, the effect on the buildings was like shaking a wicker basket. Temples, too, survived well. These were constructed using an apparently incomprehensible network of interlocking beams and crisscrossing frames which could yield in any direction. Similarly, many communities in South America would construct the lower story of stone, the upper of light wood, walled with rushes or cane. \

Such structures withstood the passage of earthquakes for centuries, but most cities today are a blend of the traditional and the modern: houses perhaps one or more hundred years old; modern buildings with several stories; and towering blocks of masonry, housing apartments and offices looming over them. As architects and engineers reach upward in the interest of saving space, the problems they set themselves in earthquake country have become more acute.

When the ground shakes, a structure will remain safe as long as stresses within the structure are below a critical point. The damage from shaking is caused by vibrations transferred from the ground to a building, which must either follow the motion of the shaking, or absorb it somehow.

There are several factors which determine the extent of damage to a building: the type of ground it is sited on; its design; the quality of its workmanship and the materials used in its construction; and most significantly, the nature of the shock to which it is exposed. A short, sharp high frequency shock lasting only a few seconds is comparatively easy for the engineer to combat. A longer shock lasting several seconds or even fractions of a minute, which is at a lower frequency and usually occurs some distance away from the epicenter of the earthquake is a different matter altogether, and can cause severe damage, even total destruction. It is the two- to four-story buildings which are most vulnerable to the short, sharp shock – taller buildings may escape almost unscathed. A longer shock may leave the lower buildings all but untouched, and set the taller ones tumbling.

One of the problems in the past has been the lack of what are called strong motion records of earthquakes. All too often the recording device itself has been so badly affected by the quake that its findings are useless. Engineers were skeptical about seismologists' theories for a long time, but this is no longer the case. Earthquake engineering as a science is in its infancy but advances are being made in the discovery of the precise forces which a building is subjected to during an earthquake.

The San Fernando earthquake of 1971 was a milestone in this new science. Previously, it had been thought that the average maximum force imposed on a building by an earthquake of moderate size was something in the order of 5 to 10 percent of gravity. In 1971, two hundred strong motion recording seismographs, or accelerographs, showed that some buildings had been exposed to peak accelerations up to and beyond that of gravity itself – the greatest was 120 percent. More recently, it was discovered that the Managua quake in Nicaragua in 1972 subjected buildings to up to 39 percent of gravity.

The comparative statistics of the two earthquakes make interesting reading, for the San Fernando quake of 6.6 magnitude led to scattered damage and the loss of sixty lives, whereas the smaller Nicaraguan quake (6.2 magnitude) flattened most of the city of Managua and killed over five thousand people.

As building codes until recently have been calculated on the premise of a probable maximum acceleration of 10 percent, the implications are clear and alarming. If a quake, even a moderate one, is close by, then buildings may be

Liquefaction. At Niigata, Japan, in 1964, the soil lost all its strength and became a soggy mess. This apartment building quietly turned on its side, so slowly that the occupants were able to walk down the outer walls to safety.

NOAA/EDS

A ten-story apartment block in Caracas, Venezuela, was totally wrecked by the 1967 earthquake.

NOAA/EDS

subjected to forces five or even ten times stronger than those allowed for in the original specifications. There is a further complication, for the duration of a shock is all-important. The longer tremors last, the more likely it is that buildings will be set in oscillation and start to swing. The shaking lasted twelve seconds in the San Fernando quake in 1971; around forty seconds in the San Francisco earthquake in 1906, and around three whole minutes in the Alaskan quake in 1964. One day seismologists may be able to predict when, and where and in what magnitude a quake might occur, but it is hard to think that they will ever be able to predict the duration of the tremor; yet in terms of construction in a seismic region, this information is vital.

The danger in a shock lasting a length of time is that a condition of resonance is set up. All structures – and parts of structures – have their natural period of vibration, which increases with height above ground. If this natural period coincides with the period of the earth tremor, in other words when the natural sway of the building is the same as that of the shock affecting it and when the whole building resonates like a huge tuning fork, the result can be catastrophic.

The cumulative effects of such a situation was brought to light during the Caracas earthquake in Venezuela in 1967. Here it was found that most buildings between ten and twelve stories high, and built on a thick alluvial base, suffered total destruction. Lower buildings survived much better. What happened was that the short period earthquake waves were soon absorbed in the soil and rock leaving the longer period ones to affect the buildings. As these passed through the ground, they were slowed down and their amplitude was increased. Alluvial soils absorb small earthquake waves, but amplify the effects of larger ones, and the thicker the alluvium the more the waves are slowed and the greater the increase in amplitude. At Caracas it was clear that the natural period of these tall buildings almost coincided with the natural period of the quake after its waves had passed through the ground.

No building is safer than the ground on which it rests, is a truism which applies to every earthquake. If the site actually straddles a fault, which moves in an earthquake, then disaster is almost inevitable. But few faults break cleanly, they usually shatter like cracking plaster. Within this fault zone, damage may be extreme, yet fractionally outside it the results of a quake may be minimal. At San Fernando, nearly one-third of the houses within the fault zone were declared unsafe, whereas the comparable figure outside the zone was one in twenty. For moderate damage the relative statistics were 80 percent and 30 percent respectively. The conclusion was that the building code then in use was inadequate for a near earthquake of even a moderate intensity.

Alluvial soil; earth fill, or what is termed "made" land, where earth, stones, and rubble have been tipped to create a firm foundation; sand, pumice, and other loose subsoils are the worst possible types of foundation for construction in a seismic zone. Such alluvial areas are not uncommon in

The perils of siting. The San Andreas
fault (shown here as a white line) runs
right through the center of this
development.
USGS

many seismic areas of the world – the West Coast of America has many
which have been subjected to extensive land development in recent years.

The Bay area of San Francisco was almost completely obliterated in 1906
except where buildings were founded on piles sunk through the upper soil
layers. The higher the water table the more exaggerated the ground motion.

In extreme cases, the soil becomes subject to a process called liquefaction
in which, because of the violent vibration of soil particles, it loses all cohesion
and turns into the consistency of mud or quicksand. In some cases the soil
becomes so liquid that it actually flows, and will then fill a topographical
depression, if one exists; or else the ground may settle locally.

Our ancestors had other ideas about the foundations of buildings. The
Temple of Diana at Ephesus was built on the edge of a marsh to ward off the
effects of earthquakes – a practice which science would interpret as having
precisely the opposite effect. The Capitol in Rome was said to have been
saved on many occasions from destruction at the hands of earthquakes by the
catacombs which underlay Rome. The Greeks as well as the Romans found
that caverns, wells and quarries had the effect of absorbing earthquake
shocks and protected the buildings above them. Capua was said to have
been saved by its wells from total destruction in an earthquake in the thir-
teenth century and an Italian authority stated that the Romans would sink

wells, to weaken the effects of earth tremors – Humboldt, the geographer, said the same of the inhabitants of San Domingo.

If a building is sited on solid rock, it is less liable to damage. Sir William Hamilton recognized this, and he wrote of the 1783 Calabrian quake, "One circumstance I particularly remarked, if two towns were situated at an equal distance from the centre (of the earthquake), the one on a hill, the other on the plain, or in a bottom, the latter had always suffered greatly more by the shocks of the earthquake than the former." He attributed this, however, to "the cause coming from beneath," rather than to any more profound understanding of earthquake shocks.

There are other dangers of a bad site. The fierce tsunami which succeeded the great Alaskan earthquake swept down upon the coasts of Washington and Oregon, causing a lot of damage, although most was reserved for Crescent City. The damage after the San Fernando quake seven years later was considerable, but it would have been worse if the lower Van Norman

80,000 people live in the valley below the Lower San Fernando Dam shown here. Had it given way during the San Fernando earthquake of 1972 – as it nearly did – America would have been faced with the worst disaster in her history.

The earthfill at Hegben Dam slumped badly during the Hegben Lake earthquake of 1959.

USGS (I.J. Witkind)

These cracks in the pavement after the Managua, Nicaragua earthquake of 1972 ran in echelon to the main fault zone.

USGS (R.D. Brown Jr.)

The San Fernando earthquake of 1971 dramatically showed that the existent building codes were inadequate in some respects. The Olive View Hospital suffered considerable damage. Three of the four fire escape towers are the end of each wing (shown here flat on the ground) collapsed, and the fourth was left hanging in space. USGS

---

Dam in Mission Hills had given way, as it threatened to do, until the water level was lowered. It was estimated that 80,000 people were placed at risk. If the dam had broken at six o'clock in the morning when the quake struck, most people would have been in bed and unable to escape the cascading waters.

Mallet had noticed that rectangular buildings with walls at right angles to the shock were more likely to be thrown down than those running parallel with it. This was particularly evident after the Managua quake in 1972 where detailed engineering research was undertaken very shortly after the first destructive tremors. Here it was found that the pattern of damage ran parallel with the principal fault in the area, which suggested that the main forces imposed on structures in the area had been in that direction – as might be expected – yet many buildings had their maximum direction of resistance away from the obvious orientation. The importance of siting and orientation is crucial – how many buildings in earthquake-prone areas should never have been built at all, least of all of the chosen type of construction or in the selected direction?

For many years seismologists, building engineers and other interested parties had put forward theories on earthquake construction and design. Their ideas and efforts were rudely put to the test at San Fernando. It was a quake which provided a lot of sober food for thought, not least that the only true test of earthquake design and earthquake building standards is during earthquake itself.

San Fernando, 1971. These freeways
under construction collapsed like a
giant's plaything.

USGS

Reports revealed that one-story houses performed better than those of
two or more, and that the floor construction of wood or solid concrete slabs
made little difference. Braced brick chimneys – in which the brickwork is
reinforced with steel strips – survived consistently, but unbraced ones
fell like ninepins. It was also reassuring that newer houses survived on the
whole better than older ones. Mobile homes, which were often poorly
braced and usually just propped on bricks or some other foundation, often
suffered damage, but this was rarely total.

One of the most awe-inspiring sights were the freeways, twisted and distorted like some giant's plaything. An improvement was clearly needed in this direction. It was frightening how the schools had failed to stand up to the tremors, although fortunately the quake had struck before the school rooms were occupied by children. Structural failure in a number of schools resulting from the Santa Barbara earthquake of 1978 showed that improvement is still needed.

It is now possible using simulated "models" and computer techniques, to

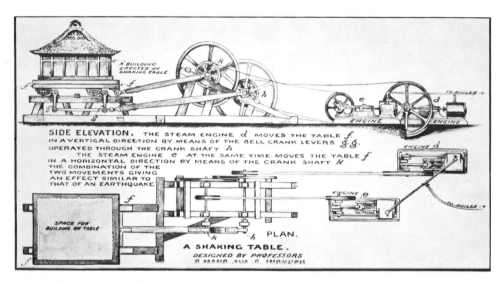

A Shaking Table. Designed in the 1920s in Japan to test buildings for earthquake resistance.

Illustrated London News

reconstruct earthquake effects. On a basis of similar earthquake magnitude, ground motions and shock duration applied to existing situations of population densities and distribution, current types of building construction and design, and the probable activity by the population at any given time, day or night, an examination of the San Fernando earthquake in 1971 came up with remarkably similar figures and statistics to those which actually occurred. A projection on the same basis of an earthquake of 8.3 magnitude striking along the San Andreas fault at varying times of day and night has produced the following conclusions:

2.30 A.M. – 2,850 deaths and 10,800 injuries leading to hospitalization.

2.00 P.M. – 9,460 deaths and 34,400 injuries.

4.30 P.M. – 10,360 deaths and 40,360 injuries.

And an earthquake along the Hayward fault would result in comparable casualties, with the added danger of dam failure and a further huge population at risk.

The problems in arriving at such figures are considerable because so many imponderable factors are involved – the siting, the magnitude of the quake, duration of tremors and the direction of maximum activity. The type of soil poses further difficulties. The type of building construction, situation, orientation and design, not to say the location of population at any given time pose others. Nevertheless, even the most skeptical must concede that, whatever doubts they might have over the detailed accuracy of such projections, it all adds up to a picture of blood-chilling dimensions.

Steel-framed buildings, having strength combined with a degree of flexibility, and which are of light mass are likely to suffer little damage. Concrete buildings with few door or window openings – which weaken the

Earthquake simulation. A modern machine for testing strength on large building structures. This particular machine was designed for use by the University of Canterbury, New Zealand, one of the principal research centers investigating the effects of earthquake forces on building material.      Dartec Ltd.

structure – are also likely to survive well, although weakness may be revealed at the joints. Hollow concrete blocks, unreinforced and unfilled may prove lethal, but if reinforced with steel ties and the hollows filled with more concrete, they perform considerably better. Ancient brick buildings especially where the brick is bound by inadequate or very sandy mortar can also be fatal to the occupants – reinforcement with steel frames is a considerable improvement. But nothing can save the vernacular adobe buildings prevalent in the Middle East and in many other parts of the world, often with heavy roofs bearing down on the thoroughly unreliable walls, and the whole held together by what one person described as spit and willpower.

Roofs themselves can be a considerable source of danger, by being too heavy for the framework below, or insecurely tied to the rest of the house. Tiled roofs are heavy and have to be supported by strong beams. Tiles are also easily dislodged and turn into sharp-sided missiles for anyone walking below – at best they may crack and let in water. Balconies and parapets can also be very dangerous. But the most frequent hazard is if the whole building is top-heavy possibly through water absorption. Many modern buildings are propped on concrete pillars with little or inadequate cross-bracing,

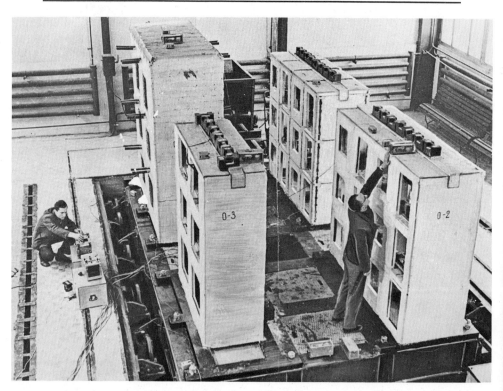

A vibration platform being used in Russia, to test structures designed for seismic regions.

Novosti Press Agency

Building failure. The collapse of the front wall of the factory left the floors completely unsupported during the Skopje earthquake in Yugoslavia, 1963.

Skopje

providing garaging space for cars below, but creating a structure doomed to fall in any but the slightest tremor.

Safety advisers recommend that in an earthquake, rather than rush into the street it is better to remain indoors – and lean against some strong inner wall, under the lintel of a door, or beneath a stout piece of furniture such as a dining room table. Most walls fall outward in an earthquake, and few towns, except the most modern have wide enough streets. These are usually blocked with rubble, which hampers rescue efforts. Even if the house fronts survive, as in Messina in 1908, the balconies, parapets, signs and other projections which are a feature in many towns and cities are usually first to go, and obliterate anything or anyone beneath.

Innumerable pitfalls and hazards in construction can endanger a building, and only constant knowledgeable supervision at all stages will reveal them. If they should slip by or escape notice, only the damage sustained as the result of an earthquake will show what had occurred, and by then it will be too late.

There is a perennial conflict among architects between "soft" buildings –

ones with slender frameworks which sway with the shock – and "stiff" ones, which rely on a solid core of heavy reinforced walls to counteract the effects of the quake by sheer strength. Variants of both types have been used and are under examination.

A recent development in earthquake construction is the use of rubber pads – alternate rubber and metal sheets bonded together. When a quake strikes, this sandwich is moved by the quake and is affected by the shock, rather than the building itself, which remains isolated from the tremors. Experiments have proved highly promising, reducing the forces imposed on a structure by a factor of as much as ten. But when all is said and done, until a real quake tests these ideas, no one can really know how effective they are.

It is impossible to remove all hazards, but it is possible to minimize them by sensible design and planning. In an earthquake, neighboring houses often pound against each other, but row houses do not, although end corner houses which are without support on one side are more vulnerable. An early traveler in Caracas in Venezuela, which has been regularly hit by earth-quakes for centuries – some of a considerable size – noted that the houses along one side of the street were bound together by iron rods, and that those on the corners of such rows had foundations which were splayed outward, rather than at strict right angles.

Indoors, stoves or heavy pieces of furniture are subject to similar forces as the building itself, unless secured to it in some way. Otherwise they are

Building failure. The failure of the central reinforced concrete columns led to the total collapse of the massive computer center in Bucharest during the earthquake of 1977.

Professor N.N. Ambraseys

Building failure. The failure of buttressing constructed of brittle material led to the collapse of roof and walls of the Gazi-Isa-Beg Mosque in Skopje, Yugoslavia. The flexible minaret stood up well to the close shock, losing only part of the upper parapet and the whole of a metal spire.

League of Red Cross Societies

liable to perform a weird and sometimes lethal dance as they career across a room, and may smash through an outer wall in their mad progress unless restrained. Wall veneers and paneling may fall off unless properly secured.

As the knowledge of the effect of earthquakes on various structures, and the experience and skill of engineers and architects in combating the remarkable stresses imposed on buildings by earth tremors have advanced,

Building failure. These modern buildings in Managua, Nicaragua after the earthquake of 1972 appear to have emerged relatively unscathed, but in fact due to non-uniform stiffness at low level there was considerable structural damage.

Lower buildings properly constructed using the local *tazakl* style—timber-braced frame with filled in brickwork —were left largely intact after the 6.2 magnitude earthquake.

EERI Managua Conference Proceedings

Building failure. The earthquake of 1975 at Lice, Turkey led to the total destruction of these houses which were of rubble masonry construction and already weakened by age and many structural alterations.

League of Red Cross Societies

various rules and codes of conduct have evolved.

The most widely used building code is the SEACOC, more commonly referred to as the California Code, which is used as the basis for a number of national earthquake building codes across the world. This is a collection of rules and parameters, updated and strengthened with each advance in scientific and engineering knowledge. The code uses the results from research in Japan, Russia, New Zealand and several other countries.

But any building code is only as strong as its enforcement. Many countries do have building codes, of varying stringency. In some instances there is no concerted control over design, or supervision of building methods and practices, or actual construction. Buildings of unsuitable size, type, construction or design, often on the wrong site, are built for reasons of economy or sheer neglect. The teamwork which is necessary in earthquake country between architect, engineer and seismologist, a cooperation which might mean the difference between life and death, is often lacking altogether and at other times is an uneasy one.

A builder in earthquake country is faced with a perpetual conflict. In the first place he must build a structure which is economically and environmentally acceptable, as regards cost, design and position; and on the other hand he must build to withstand the potential strains of an earthquake. The building codes of many countries are *minimum* requirements. Even at that level they are expensive. To make codes more stringent would cost more money and might make a whole development uneconomic. This remains a constant dilemma. The Californian code cannot be applied in every area. Subsoil varies; local materials differ in quality and type from those recommended in the code; standards of construction and builders' skill may not be of the highest class; enforcement and supervision may be lacking. There are plenty of opportunities for graft and corruption. Examples of the subtle use of the blind eye are legion. The whole leads up to a huge gamble with the forces of nature.

The philosophy behind earthquake construction is that saving lives is of paramount importance. Buildings should be able to resist minor quakes without damage, moderate ones with some damage, and survive major quakes without collapse but with an acceptable degree of structural damage. Some buildings are in a separate category – such as hospitals, schools and power stations – and these must not only remain standing, they must also remain functional after an earthquake.

The true results of an earthquake cannot just be measured in terms of casualties. The loss in terms of the human suffering of survivors may be colossal, and the loss in insurance terms enormous. In Managua for instance, many buildings did not collapse and the residents walked out alive and thus they served their primary function, but the structural damage was so severe that in many cases the buildings were beyond economic repair.

Not only small, poor nations are economically threatened by earthquakes.

A modern earthquake-resistant
eleven-story building in Kazakhstan,
USSR.

Novosti Press Agency

It has been calculated that should there be a repeat of the Kanto earthquake of 1923, on the same site and of the same magnitude, the effect on the Japanese economy would be staggering. To start with, the gross national product would drop by about 15 percent. The financial structure of Tokyo would be faced with total disruption – after the Kanto quake it was estimated that 18 percent of bills became unpayable. A comparable situation today would lead to incredible rates of inflation as depositors tried to withdraw their savings to rebuild. This in turn would lead to prices practically doubling, industrial production declining, unemployment soaring to close on five million – with all its attendant economic and social strains – and

This beautiful 42-story building houses the Tokyo headquarters of the Yasuda Fire and Marine Insurance Company, and incorporates the most up-to-date earthquake-resistant techniques.

Yasuda Fire and Marine Insurance Company

living standards reduced by a half. In short, Japan might lurch in a matter of weeks or months from being one of the world's richest countries to being one of the poorest.

With our increasing knowledge of the nature of earthquakes and the awesome power of nature which we can neither infallibly predict nor control, it would be sensible, one might suppose, to avoid building on sites particularly prone to earthquakes. Yet this is not the case. In many parts of the world, man has built only to see his buildings demolished; has rebuilt and seen the whole sorry affair repeated. Concepcion in Chile has been destroyed more than five times. Messina has arisen again and again. Antioch was

The Trans-America building in San Francisco. A modern earthquake- engineered structure.

subjected to at least nine major earthquakes in recorded history. "The Truth," as one seventeenth century writer put it, "is our Cities are built upon Ruines and our Fields and Countries stand upon broken Arches and Vaults."

Sometimes the reasons for rebuilding on the same site are the same ones which prompted the founding of the city in the first place – often economic or defense considerations. Sometimes the sheer perversity of human nature, or a refusal to be driven from a spot which one has come to know and love is responsible. Often it is a matter of civic and personal pride. But the risks the people who choose to live in these places take should not be dismissed – it is a risk – a risk to lives, to property, to peace of mind, and to the fragile civilized fabric people make of their existences in their own communities.

In an excellent book *Peace of Mind in Earthquake Country*, Peter Yanev outlines the risks of the twenty million who live in California, where few of the main population areas are far from an active fault, and many major communities are less than twenty miles from a fault which is known to have been active in living memory. Yet people will doubtless go on living there, even after the "Big One" comes.

# 8
# The Age of Prediction

A BELIEF IN "earthquake weather" is one that goes back for thousands of years. Man, floundering in an element which to him was wholly incomprehensible, grasped at any straw which would provide some rational explanation of the earthquake phenomenon. It seemed inconceivable that nature gave no indication of what it was doing, and the weather seemed the natural way to forecast such an event.

Pliny the Elder – who perished on the slopes of Vesuvius after examining the volcanic process too closely – had declared that "tremors of the earth never occur except when the sea is calm and sky so still that birds are unable to soar because all the breath that carries them has been withdrawn; and never except after wind, doubtless because then the blast has been shut up in the veins and hidden hollows of the sky." Pausanius, one hundred and fifty years later, believed that continuous rainstorms or draughts, hot winters, hazy sun in summer and blasts of wind swooping upon the land and overturning trees – which hedged his bets pretty well – were sure signs that an earthquake was impending.

Many centuries later, the Reverend Stukeley stated that earthquakes were accompanied and preceded by high winds, fireballs and meteors, and by a continually clouded sun; that they usually occurred in calm weather with a black cloud or when rain had followed a great drought; and he added that they were succeeded by plague, contagious diseases and famines. Some said that earthquakes were preceded by and ended with a hard frost, while others supported the theory that lightning flashed across the sky before a quake – as a sure sign of God's wrath. There were few who did not believe that certain weather conditions could "trigger" an earthquake.

Those who believed they could forecast an earthquake usually found ample evidence after the event to support their case. After the 1750 London quake it was remembered that there had been many natural phenomena which took place that winter. New Year's Day had been heralded by a remarkable display of Northern Lights, which was seen as far south as London – with, ominously, now they thought about it, many blood red shades. Early in February a bad electric storm occurred at Bristol, which resulted in no loss of life but caused a great deal of damage. This occurrence was eagerly pounced on by the religious as yet another example of God's fury.

"Earthquake weather" was usually described as eerily still, and occurred principally in the autumn and spring. Thin streaks of cloud in an otherwise clear sky and a hazy sun, presaged an earthquake. Today, in Japan, there is a 77-year-old man who predicts earthquakes by a strange rainbow which appears in the sky a few hours before the tremor happens – the paler the colors, the stronger the quake. He has a number of accurate predictions to his credit, including a forecast of the great Kanto Plain earthquake of 1923. Another Japanese sage believes that merely by glancing at the sky he can recognize "earthquake clouds," thin wispy clouds like aircraft vapor trails.

There are other popular indicators. Some people believe they can "smell" earthquakes; others say they can predict quakes from a peculiar feeling in their stomachs. The Ancient Egyptians and the Chaldeans also had the power of prediction, as have members of other civilizations at various times or so it is alleged. Few claims can match the pomposity of magistrates in a small town in Mexico who prevented panicking people from leaving town by threatening heavy fines or imprisonment, grandiloquently declaring that "the magistracy in their wisdom will be well aware of the period of real and imminent danger. Should it arise, they will give orders for flight."

But certain people do seem to have the ability to warn of impending danger. The case is told of a priest who ran through the streets of Lima before one devastating earthquake calling on people to repent of their sins before it was too late. Elsewhere in South America, *tembloron*, as they were known, who possessed a kind of seismic second sight, were truly believed to be able to predict quakes. There are also many stories of people suddenly getting up and walking to safety before a quake occurs. When asked why, they reply that they do not know, they just felt that they had to leave the house or room in which they had been.

A small boy in Bucharest in 1940 had been put to bed, when suddenly his parents saw him walking downstairs. When asked why he had woken up, he said he did not know, he just felt he had to. Moments later the quake struck and the room in which he had been sleeping was destroyed.

Water phenomena are more reliable and these are now being closely studied as possible earthquake indicators. On one occasion the Capuchin Fathers at Melfi noticed that the water in a nearby lake was foaming and gave timely warning of an earthquake. The famous hotsprings at Adepsus and Thermopylae stopped bubbling shortly before a major quake in Northern Greece. Before the Lisbon earthquake, well levels in many parts of Portugal and Spain behaved in a peculiar way, rising and falling for no apparent reason and with no pattern. In Calabria before the 1783 quakes, peculiar "boiling" was reported at sea and a local fish, the *cicirelli*, a great delicacy but usually

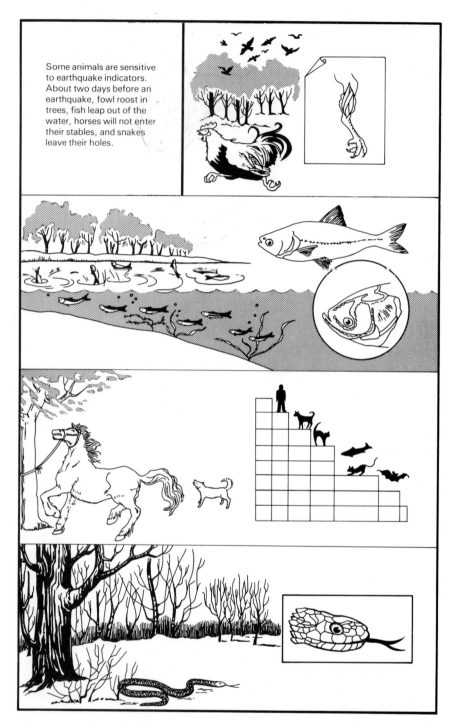

Some animals are sensitive to earthquake indicators. About two days before an earthquake, fowl roost in trees, fish leap out of the water, horses will not enter their stables, and snakes leave their holes.

This graphic series of illustrations in a Chinese magazine shows what are believed to be the most sensitive regions in the anatomies of various creatures. A scale shows relative sensitivities – from the bat, which is the most sensitive, to the human, who is almost insensitive by comparison.

found only in deep water, were caught in large numbers near the surface. The Catfish Society in Japan, a group of water-level observers, are credited with a number of successful predictions. They take their name from the legendary catfish once believed to produce earthquakes in Japan. The society has found that a gradual rise of well levels takes place some days in advance of a quake, and then suddenly drops again a few hours before the first tremors.

In the animal world recent and exciting strides have been made in earthquake prediction. The early tales of animals showing increasing restlessness before an earthquake were largely discounted as the imaginings of terrified inhabitants suffering from the after effects of a disaster. Now these old theories are being taken very seriously. The Chinese and the Japanese are foremost in the study of what are called animal precursors.

Observations that animals behave in peculiar fashion before an earthquake have been noticed for a long time. A Roman philosopher pointed out that sailors could anticipate earthquakes by observing seabirds. The birds seemed unable to fly; others hid their heads under their wings. Sir William Hamilton noted during his study of the Calabrian earthquake, "I was assured that all animals and birds in a greater or less degree were much more sensible of an approaching shock of an earthquake than any human being, but that geese, above all, seem to be the soonest and most alarmed at the approach of a shock, if in water they quit it immediately, and there are no means of driving them into water for some time."

Zoo and domestic animals are often observed behaving in an odd way before an earthquake. They appear frightened, uneasy and abnormally jumpy. Wild animals and reptiles are also affected – rats and snakes come out of their holes – snakes appeared above ground during the winter in China before one drastic quake and froze to death. Nocturnal animals come out in the daytime. Indians living on the banks of the Orinoco River, noticed that crocodiles which are normally silent, would run with wild cries into the forest on the approach of a tremor.

Pheasants seem to provide the most promising study for animal earthquake prediction research. A Japanese seismologist in 1923 noticed some pheasants screaming and obviously in a state of alarm in a large garden near his house, before the great earthquake that destroyed much of Tokyo and Yokohama. Now pheasants are studied extensively by the Chinese, and several other nations.

Fish also give considerable promise as precursors of earthquakes. Sharks are notoriously sensitive to impulses beyond the range of human faculties, and sea mammals, such as whales and dolphins, could be equally useful. A dramatic incident occurred before the recent Guatemala quake, when a man sitting quietly in his chair was astonished to see a gold fish in a bowl suddenly shoot from the water and land at his feet. Mystified, he returned the fish to the water, and shortly afterward the Guatemala quake of 1976 struck.

Experiments are under way in many countries into all aspects of these animal phenomena. One experiment by the University of California is proceeding near the peculiar "Palmdale Bulge," where some mice have been put in artificial burrows, and cages of kangaroo rats are placed above ground. Avid rodent-watchers study every twitch of their whiskers.

A conference in October, 1976, the first of its kind, discussed the abnormal behavior of animals in earthquake areas, and a number of theories were put forward as to why animals were able to sense the coming of earthquakes better than man.

One possible explanation lies in the idea that before an earthquake happens certain changes take place in the earth's magnetic field – sharks and some other creatures are particularly sensitive to this. The emission of sounds beyond or below the range of human hearing, was also put forward as a cause of disturbance. It is known that under stress the properties of rocks can change in a pronounced way, and some delegates felt that it was this underground straining that the animals could detect. This is a fascinating area of study, and one barely explored. Animal behavior may soon provide a credible means of predicting earthquakes.

Foreshocks of varying intensity and extending over varying lengths of time usually precede an earthquake. This is occasionally a fruitful source of prediction of a major quake, but on other occasions, the foreshocks seem to presage nothing in particular, and eventually fizzle out. Taken by themselves they are inconclusive, but in conjunction with other precursors, they can be significant.

Research into geological precursors of earthquakes is being carried out in many centers in many countries. Among these, some of the most promising areas of study are land deformation, tilt, and strain – it was discovered afterward that the great Japanese quake of 1923 had been preceded by quite considerable land tilting. There was similar tilting in California before the 1971 earthquake, but no one recognized it. Changes in the velocity of sound transmitted through rocks, fluctuations in local magnetic fields, variations in the electrical properties of rocks are other geological disturbances which are being studied.

The discharge of gases from rocks, principally the heavy gas radon, which is believed to be squeezed out by crustal compression, is being actively investigated, particularly in Russia where this particular theory originated. It was noticed that shortly before an earthquake the radon content in wells rose dramatically. Another Russian theory is based on evidence of a distinct and remarkable difference between the relative speeds of the P and S waves on the ground prior to a quake, and the return to normal shortly before the quake itself. Interest in these Russian advances was aroused during a scientific interchange in 1971, when it was discovered that for the previous twenty-five years the Russians had been carrying out extensive and exhaustive tests in the Tadzhikistan region, and coming up with some very remarkable results.

Seismologists believe that certainty in prediction is a little nearer. Yet inexplicable variations do occur. Sometimes one recording station will register nothing, yet one equally distant from the shock will show dramatic seismic movement. But when reliable earthquake prediction becomes an accomplished fact, it will be the greatest advance in the earth sciences since the evolution of the tectonic plate theory.

One of the problems in the historical study of earthquakes is that only in very few countries, such as China and Japan, do reasonably accurate records go back very far. Elsewhere, records have only been kept for a few centuries. Nor are many of these records necessarily completely reliable. The time and location of an earthquake can be and often is widely exaggerated and extensive detective work is often necessary before anything resembling an earthquake history can be built up for a given area. This work often reveals that parts of the world, up to now considered almost seismically quiescent, have in past centuries been subjected to considerable seismic activity which has gone unnoticed as there was no one present able or willing to record what had happened.

However, despite this lack of reliable evidence, study of past earthquakes has revealed another interesting phenomenon, which has led to what is known as the "gap" theory. In many parts of the world, along major fault lines, earthquakes have sometimes occurred in a form of logical sequence. Epicentral locations show that stress has accumulated over a long period of time along a fault, until released by an earthquake. A while later, another earthquake may take place, perhaps some hundreds of miles away, while between them appears a "gap" which gives every indication that one day an earthquake will occur here to complete the sequence.

There are several of these gaps. There are two in Alaska – the Sitka quake took place in a more easterly one in 1972. The San Andreas fault has a number of ominous "gaps," and it was the gap theory which led to the increasing and finally immense effort the Chinese made in the early 1970s, which resulted in the correct prediction of the colossal Liaoning Earthquake of 1975, where prompt action saved the lives of countless thousands. This was an extraordinary achievement in the history of man's bitter association with earthquakes.

In 1966 it was decided in China to start a major national effort mobilizing the masses for earthquake prediction. Under the slogan "Rather a thousand days with no earthquake than one day with no precaution," groups were set up under local brigades with the tasks of watching easily identified earthquake precursors – zoo and domestic animals, the radon emission and water levels. Groups and individuals were under instruction only to report when something abnormal occurred. A massive army of over 300,000 amateur earthquake-watchers was established. As a result of this effort a number of earthquakes were predicted, with some mistakes to start with, but gradually the system was perfected.

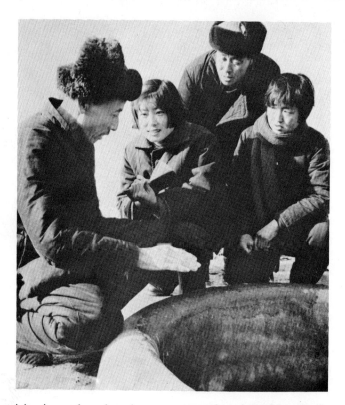

Mass participation and earthquake education form the basis of China's attempt to find a way to predict earthquakes reliably. Over 300,000 volunteer helpers watch for earthquake precursors. These efforts have already resulted in the correct prediction of an earthquake at Liaoning in 1975 which saved countless lives, but a quake the following year at Tangshan which was not predicted is believed to have killed over 650,000 people. This farmer and his family are observing the water level in his well.

It was early in 1970 that a rather ominous "gap" was spotted in the earthquake pattern in northeast China, in the province of Liaoning. In this vast province of a quarter million square miles (0.65 million sq km), bounded on the west by Hopeh province, and Inner Mongolia, and on the east by Korea, lay a densely populated and industrialized portion of China with a population of nearly thirty-four million people. There had been a number of earthquakes to the south; in 1966 at Hsingtai, 600 miles (966 km) south, the following year at Hochien and in 1969 at Pohai Bay, only 250 miles (403 km) away. There seemed a definite gradual migration to the northeast. This indication was so pronounced that it was decided that Liaoning Province should be declared an area "deserving special seismological and geophysical attention," and the two seismic stations in the province were rapidly augmented.

By mid-1974 a number of highly significant factors began to emerge.

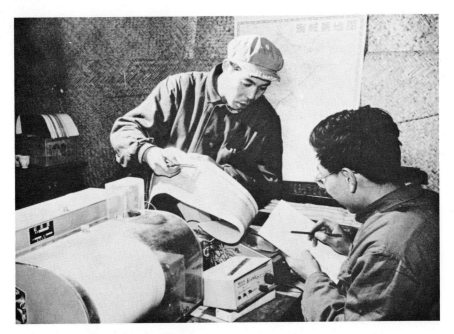

Reports are collected and collated
at centers throughout the region.

Amongst other things it was found that a number of small faults were active, that considerable uplift in the area had been continuing for nearly twenty years and that local tilting was more pronounced, and also there was a steady increase in the incidence of small quakes. In June that year a medium-term prediction was made of a 5–6 magnitude shock within the next one to two years, and local organizations were brought into the picture. It was their task to promote earthquake education and understanding, activate prediction groups at village level, encourage those watching water levels, and disseminate disaster prevention techniques. As a result, several thousand amateur posts were set up and amateur effort brought to a high pitch of alertness.

The precursors continued to strengthen. Early in January 1975 a short-term prediction of a 5.5–6.0 magnitude earthquake in the first six months of the year was declared, and it was noticed that the tilting which had been going on for a number of years had suddenly reversed. The first small foreshock occurred on February 1, and others continued with rising frequency for the next two days. Then, suddenly, all went quiet. On February 4 it was declared that an earthquake was imminent. Early that afternoon final emergency preparations were put in hand and wholesale evacuation took place. At five o'clock, a quake which wrecked 90 percent of the city of Haicheng and did a great deal of other damage broke across the province. Effects to intensity IX were experienced across 386 square miles (1,000 sq km). The extent of the casualties was not revealed but it was considerably less than would otherwise have occurred.

This can be considered a classic case of earthquake prediction, and it will be interesting to see how often it will be emulated. The precautions and system certainly saved thousands of lives. But could it be done in a western country? The essence of the Chinese technique was first a process of understanding to promote cooperation, and then local initiative was stimulated for maximum participation. Intelligent anticipation followed with all authorities alerted, local plans clear and well prepared, and relief services outside the expected affected area standing by with immediate medical and other relief.

There have been four successful earthquake predictions in China in recent years, but a fifth, the catastrophic quake of 1976 at Tangshan somehow slipped through the seismological net. Why? No one knows for certain. The quake was expected. Long-term and medium-term indicators clearly showed that one was due in the fairly near future, but there were no more specific indications than that. It is obviously wholly impracticable to evacuate towns and villages, or entire populations on the off chance that something might happen in the next month or so. In this instance the short-term warnings were not detected – if indeed there were any – and the number of casualties has never been revealed, but some observers think that it might well exceed half a *million* people. Yet the failure of the system to predict the Tangshan disaster should not be allowed to detract from the equally significant success at Liaoning. Here people's lives were saved, the province was largely preserved without total dislocation and, perhaps most important of all, the effects of the earthquakes were minimized by the personal activity of individuals.

It seems unlikely, certainly in the short-term, that one specific indicator can be relied upon to predict an earthquake. Rather, an accumulation of evidence from many different sources will reveal that the balance of probability is that an earthquake will take place imminently. There might always be a nagging fear that the seismologists could be wrong. False alarms would do more to destroy the credibility of the system than anything else. If a similar situation as that which occurred in Hawaii with false tsunami warnings took place with earthquake prediction in San Francisco or Los Angeles, no one would listen and that could be disastrous.

The United States Geological Survey was appointed as the leading agency in the collection of earthquake prediction, but it is now proposed to set up a National Earthquake Prediction Council to coordinate research into all aspects of earthquake prediction and hazard reduction which is currently undertaken by eight different federal departments. It would be the responsibility of the council to warn the governor of a threatened state of specific earthquake hazard and prediction.

Following the San Fernando earthquake of 1971, it was concluded that ten separate metropolitan areas were most at risk within the United States. These are: San Francisco, Los Angeles, Salt Lake City – Ogden, Puget Sound, Hawaii, St. Louis – Memphis, Anchorage, Fairbanks, Boston,

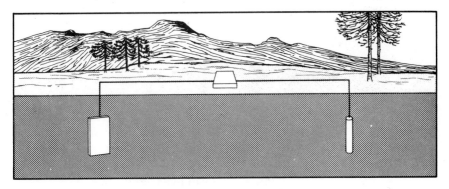

In order to try to rob the earthquake of its mystery and show that people by their own efforts can do much to save their own lives, the Chinese distribute simple scientific instruments as part of a broader campaign of earthquake education. Here an "earth-meter" can record any alteration in the electric conductivity in the ground.

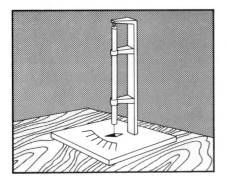

This simple magnet suspended on a thread will show any change in the magnetic field.

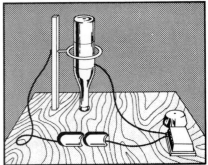

Earthquake warning device. When the inverted bottle is jogged it will fall over and set the bell ringing.

Buffalo and Charleston, South Carolina. Yet of these threatened communities, little work has gone on except in the first two, and few states except California have taken extensive measures to reduce earthquake hazard.

There have been a number of highly successful predictions of small seismological events in various parts of the United States in recent years. This has led to the belief that earthquakes do give precise warnings of their approach, if these can be spotted in time, and it is believed that in the event of a 6.0 magnitude quake advance anomalies might be evident several months in advance; for one of 7.0 magnitude they might be evident up to three years before, and that with an 8.0 magnitude earthquake this time factor might stretch to a decade or more. However, instruments have to be in the right place at the right time. Ironically, a state of affairs is emerging similar to what used to happen in the early days of earthquake reporting, for information will only be recorded if adequate resources are allotted in the first place to the right areas. This parallels old beliefs that there were no earthquakes in many areas of the world – for the simple reason that no one lived there to report them. Great stretches of the globe were assumed to be nonseismic, when the reverse in fact was true.

The social consequence of earthquake warnings is a subject receiving increasing attention. A recent study at the University of Colorado's Institute of Behavioral Studies, in which hundreds of businessmen, families and other groups in the earthquake zone of California were consulted, came up with the conclusion that "unless planning is begun now to prevent it, the first credible earthquake prediction . . . will exact a very high price in economic dislocation and social disruption."

The false alarm, or the not-so-false alarm, a penalty of the inexact science which earthquake prediction is, could cause severe disturbance. If human lives were not involved, cynics might be inclined to think that it would be better *not* to know of a forthcoming earthquake.

In the search for reliable earthquake indicators, as in many other fields, the wheel has come full circle. Once again the old philosophers' theories are being disinterred, dusted down and dressed in modern scientific clothes. The influence of the moon and the planets is gaining increasing credibility. It was Sir Isaac Newton who forecast that in 1750 the planet Jupiter would be abnormally close to the earth, and severe upsets might result. Now the planetary alignments during and before the great earthquakes of history are coming under scrutiny. This has led to the authors of a recent book *The Jupiter Effect* to point out that unusual planetary alignments are going to occur during the next ten years and that this points to a considerable increase in earthquake activity.

Another branch of earthquake prediction, risk prediction, is carried out by insurance companies in order to assess the risk potential of an area. Although primarily for the use of insurance companies, their computer simulations have a major bearing on town design, earthquake engineering and disaster planning. By using such information, the risk manager can assess and give a rough estimate of the probable damage likely to occur in an earthquake in any given location, an estimate based on distance from the likely epicenters and the general types of construction of buildings as well as the subsoil they are sited upon. The insurance manager is then able to insist on improved foundations, additional bracing of existing walls, or other modifications. This type of prediction carries huge potential for saving lives and property.

But when all is said and done, accurate, reliable, credible, and certainly infallible earthquake prediction is still a long way off.

# 9
# Prevention and Control

FOR CENTURIES, and in many civilizations, prophets, men of "science" and others have proposed ways of preventing this scourge of the Almighty. A sixteenth-century Italian, Galesius, recommended praying to God and, in order to cover every eventuality, proposed the more heathen precaution of placing statues of the gods Mercury and Saturn on the walls of each dwelling.

After an earthquake in Scotland in 1608, rather a minor one, those in the south attributed it to the "extraordinar drouth in the summer and winter before." But their neighbors in the north were not so deceived. The Kirk in Aberdeen declared that this was a "document that God is angry against this land and against this city in particular for the manifold sins of the people." This was narrowed to one sin in particular – the sin of fishing for salmon in the nearby River Dee on the Sabbath. The sinful ones were called on to desist from this activity which had been pursued for decades with no other visible indication of divine wrath that anyone could recall. Some did, but others, as the chronicle sadly noted "plainly refusit to forbear." There have been other instances of attempting to prevent earthquakes by the power of prayer or by the elimination of some supposedly aggravating pursuit. After Port Royal had been largely destroyed in 1692, and visited again by an earthquake twenty years later, a day was set aside for abstinence and fasting in the hope of warding off further earthquakes – a practice which was continued for 150 years. After the quake of 1786 when much of the Sicilian town of Palermo was destroyed, the people walked in procession scourging themselves. Massed prayer has also been recommended. Some people feel that the concentrated thoughts of a large group can prevent an earthquake. This may be true, but it would be very hard to prove. Other attempts to control or prevent earthquakes have been suggested at various times in history. One of the most bizarre was the suggestion of "earthquake pills" which were being dispensed by a man of "medicine" during the 1750 scare in London.

For centuries the idea of controlling earthquakes was considered fanciful in the extreme, a dream which would never become practical. But recent developments point to the fact that this may really one day become a reality.

Curiously, this great advance in earthquake study came about by chance. In 1966, an area where earthquakes were rare was suddenly shaken by a series of small tremors which continued for a considerable time. Investigation showed that the beginning of this phenomenon and its continuance appeared to be directly connected with the disposal of many millions of tons of fluid waste from the manufacture of nerve gas down a couple of deep bore holes in Colorado. At first this preposterous suggestion was disputed, but seismographical records indicated differently. The disposal was stopped, and almost immediately the incidence of tremors stopped too – it started up again later, but seismologists and geologists think that this was due to the residue of the fluid already pumped into the area where a fault was located. It seemed almost unbelievable but what appeared to be happening was that the fault was actually being lubricated by the injection of the fluid.

With this evidence, previous examples of possible ground lubrication as a cause of local ground tremors were examined. The incidence of increased earthquake activity after the construction of dams and reservoirs had been attributed up to then to the great weight of the water bearing down on the underlying rocks. Now it seemed at least possible that the real cause of these "new" earthquakes in formerly earthquake-free zones might be due to lubrication instead.

For centuries, earthquakes were mysterious phenomena seemingly beyond human comprehension. Today, we understand more why earthquakes happen, and can document their effects on human communities and the natural world. One day, perhaps, we will be able to prevent them. (A sixteenth-century woodcut showing an earthquake.)

Radio Times Hulton Picture Library

There were quite a number of examples to choose from. In 1929 a reservoir in Greece was filled and immediately a number of small quakes took place, culminating in one of magnitude 5.0 nine years after the filling had commenced. Six years later the Boulder Dam project blocked the Colorado River and started to fill Lake Mead; and as the filling process continued, so seismic activity increased.

It was also conjectured that the frequency of small earth tremors found in various parts of the world, particularly in the foothills of the Himalayas, was directly related to the flood conditions of rivers. There were other incidents in various parts of the world which would fit into a similar pattern.

Oil field engineers had also noticed that the injection of water into wells sometimes had the effect of arousing small earthquakes. Now the seismologists examined the evidence. In 1969 instruments were set up in the Rangeley Oil Fields in Colorado. Here, in order to extract the last drop of oil from previously unproductive wells, water was being injected at high pressure. As the water was pumped in, seismic activity increased dramatically. Three years later in an experiment, water was pumped out of these same wells and the tremor activity dropped off significantly and then ceased altogether. It was a remarkable discovery.

Was what had been discovered a form of seismic safety valve, a means of turning earthquakes on and off? Some scientists believe that by inducing "controlled" earthquakes along a known fault it might be possible to ease the accumulating tension and stress in the rocks beneath. If it were possible by removing water to "lock" a fault, two such "locks" along a length of fault and an induced quake in the middle might satisfactorily release all the built-up stresses. It is a fascinating theory, and the experiment has been tried successfully on minor and previously inactive faults. But who is to know the interacting forces of neighboring faults? An experiment may go wrong and cause damage or loss of life. These are just two of the problems facing the exponents of induced seismicity.

We are not yet able to predict credibly. We cannot control or prevent earthquakes, but few would disagree with Count Francesco Ippolito, writing to Sir William Hamilton after the Calabrian Earthquake of 1783, "God grant that the pillars of the earth may be again fastened, and the equilibrium of both natural and moral things restored."

# Appendices

### The Modified Mercalli scale of earthquake intensity

I Not felt except by a very few, under especially favorable circumstances.

II Felt only by a few persons at rest, especially on upper floors of buildings. Delicately suspended objects may swing.

III Felt quite noticeably indoors, especially on upper floors of buildings, but many people do not recognize it as an earthquake. Standing motor cars may rock slightly. Vibration like passing truck. Duration estimated.

IV Felt indoors by many, outdoors by few. At night, some awakened. Dishes, windows, doors disturbed. Walls creak. Sensation like heavy truck striking building. Standing motor cars rock noticeably.

V Felt by nearly everyone. Some dishes, windows etc. broken. A few instances of cracked plaster. Unstable objects overturned. Disturbances of trees, poles, and other tall objects sometimes noticed. Pendulum clocks may stop.

VI Felt by all. Many frightened and run outdoors. Some heavy furniture moved. A few instances of fallen plaster or damaged chimneys.

VII Everybody runs outdoors. Damage negligible in buildings of good design and construction; slight to moderate in well-built ordinary structures; considerable in poorly built or badly designed structures; some chimneys broken. Noticed by persons driving motor cars.

VIII Damage slight in specially designed structures; considerable in ordinary substantial buildings, with partial collapse; great in poorly built structures. Panel walls thrown out of frame structures. Fall of chimneys, factory stacks, columns, monuments, walls. Heavy furniture overturned. Sand and mud ejected in small amounts. Changes in well water. Disturbs persons driving in motor cars.

IX Damage considerable in specially designed structures; well-designed frame structures thrown out of plumb; great in substantial buildings, with partial collapse. Buildings shifted off foundations. Ground clearly cracked. Underground pipes broken.

X Some well-built, wooden structures destroyed; most masonry and frame structures destroyed with foundations; ground badly cracked. Rails bent. Landslides considerable from river banks and steep slopes. Shifted sand and mud. Water splashed over banks.

XI Few masonry structures remain standing. Bridges destroyed. Broad fissures in ground. Underground pipelines out of service. Earth slumps and land slips in soft ground. Rails bent.

XII Damage total. Waves seen on ground surfaces. Lines of sight and level distorted. Objects thrown upward into the air.


## APPENDIX B

### Earthquake Terminology

Epicenter Point on the surface immediately above the focus.

Focus Underground point, or points of seismic disturbance.

Focal depth Distance measured vertically in kilometers between the focus and the epicenter.

Intensity Degree of shaking at a specific point during an earthquake. This is measured on a scale, usually the Modified Mercalli, and indicated by Roman numerals from I to XII. (See Appendix A.)

Magnitude The rating of a given earthquake, expressing the amount of energy released by an earthquake in the form of elastic waves as measured from seismograph records. The scale commonly employed is the Richter scale.

Seismograph An instrument which records a permanent and continuous record of earthwave motion.

Seismoscope An instrument which indicates the occurrence of an earthquake, but which does not permanently record it.


## APPENDIX C

### Chronology of major earthquakes referred to in the text

A.D. 63 Pompeii and Herculaneum

1556 Shenshu, China (830,000 killed – the largest earthquake toll in history)

1580 England

1692 Port Royal, Jamaica

1692 East Anglia, England

1730–1 Chile

1750 London, England

1755 Lisbon, Portugal

1755 Boston, Massachusetts

1783 Calabria, Italy

1811–2 New Madrid, Missouri

1819 India

1835 Concepcion, Chile

1857 Naples, Italy

1865 Lima, Peru

1872 Owens Valley, California

1883 [Eruption of Krakatoa]

1886 Charleston, South Carolina

1891 Mino-Owari, Japan

1899 Yakutat, Alaska (8.6 magnitude)

1902 [Eruption of Mount Pelée]

1906 San Francisco, California (7.9 magnitude, formerly classified as 8.3)

1907 Jamaica

1908 Messina, Sicily (7.5 magnitude)

1920 Kansu, China (8.6 magnitude; 180,000 killed)

1923 Kanto Plain, Japan (8.3 magnitude; killed 150,000, destroyed Tokyo and Yokohama)

1931 North Sea, England (8.0 magnitude)

1933 Long Beach, California (6.3 magnitude)

1946 Aleutian Islands (7.4 magnitude; led to tsunami in Hawaii)

1952 Kern County, California (7.7 magnitude)

1960 Chile (9.5 magnitude, formerly classified as 8.6; considerable tsunami damage across the Pacific)

1960 Agadir, Morocco (5.7 magnitude)

1963 Skopje, Yugoslavia (6.0 magnitude)

1964 Alaska (9.2 magnitude, formerly classified as 8.3)

1964 Niigata, Japan (7.5 magnitude)

1967 Caracas, Venezuela (6.5 magnitude)

1971 San Fernando, California (6.6 magnitude)

1972 Managua, Nicaragua (6.2 magnitude)

1975 Liaoning, China (7.3 magnitude)

1976 Guatemala (7.5 magnitude)

1976 Friuli, Italy (6.5 magnitude)

1976 Tangshan, China (7.6 magnitude; 650,000 believed killed)

1977 Bucharest, Rumania (7.2 magnitude)

1978 Salonika, Greece (6.5 magnitude)

1978 Miyogi, Japan (7.5 magnitude)

1978 Santa Barbara, California (5.1 magnitude)

# Bibliography

## General

ADAMS, F. D. The Birth and Development of the Geological Sciences (Williams and Wilkins 1938)

AMERICAN GEOLOGIST

The AMERICAN JOURNAL OF SCIENCE

The AMERICAN MAGAZINE

ANDREWS, A. Earthquake (Robertson 1963)

ATLANTIC MONTHLY

BEVIS, J. The History and Philosophy of Earthquakes (1757)

BRADLEY, J. Travels in the Interior of America (1809–11)

BUFFON, COMTE DE Histoire Naturelle (1749–1804)

BUSCH, N. F. Two Minutes to Noon—Tokyo 1923 (Barker 1963)

CALDER, N. R. Restless Earth (Viking Press and British Broadcasting Corporation 1972)

CHURCHILL, A. and S. Voyages (1704)

CORSON, J. P. Agadir (1960)

CROUCH, N. The General History of Earthquakes (1694)

DARWIN, C. The Geology of the Voyage of the *Beagle* (1842–6)

DAVISON, C. The Founders of Seismology (Cambridge University Press 1927)

DE NEVI, D. Earthquakes (Celestial Arts 1977)

DOOLITTLE, T. Earthquakes Explained (1693)

EARTHQUAKE RESEARCH INSTITUTE, Tokyo Bulletin

EIBY, G. A. Earthquakes (Muller 1967)

FRIED, J. J. Life Along the San Andreas Fault (Saturday Review Press/ Dutton 1973)

The GENTLEMAN'S MAGAZINE

GREY, Z. A Chronological Account of Earthquakes (1750–6)

GRIBBIN, J. and PLAGEMAN, S. H. The Jupiter Effect (Walker 1974)

HALACY, D. S. Earthquakes, a Natural History (Bobbs-Merrill 1974)

IACOPI, R. Earthquake Country (Lane Books 1971)

KENDRICK, T. D. The Great Lisbon Earthquake (Methuen 1956)

KIRCHNER, A. The Vulcanos (1669)

The LONDON MAGAZINE

LYELL, SIR CHARLES A Second Visit to the United States of North America (1849)

LYELL, SIR CHARLES Elements of Geology (1865)

LYELL, SIR CHARLES Principles of Geology (1875)

MALLET, R. A Manual of Scientific Enquiry (1849)

MALLET, R. The Great Neapolitan Earthquake of 1857 (1862)

MICHELL, J. Conjectures—The Lisbon Earthquake (1760)

MILNE, J. Earthquakes (The International Scientific Senes 1886)

NATIONAL GEOGRAPHIC MAGAZINE

NATURE

NEW SCIENTIST

NIDDRIE, D. L. When the Earth Shook (Hollis and Carter 1961)

OVERLAND MONTHLY

PERREY, A. Propositions sur les Tremblements de Terre (1863)

The PHILOSOPHICAL MAGAZINE

PINKERTON, J. Voyages and Travels (1808–14)

POPULAR SCIENCE MONTHLY

The QUARTERLY REVIEW

The ROYAL GEOGRAPHICAL SOCIETY, Journal

The ROYAL SOCIETY, Philosophical Transactions

SCIENCE

SCIENTIFIC AMERICAN

SEISMOLOGICAL SOCIETY OF AMERICA, Bulletin

SEISMOLOGICAL SOCIETY OF JAPAN, Transactions

STUKELEY, REV. W. A Philosophy of Earthquakes (1750)

SUTHERLAND, M. The San Francisco Disaster (Barrie and Rockliff 1959)

THOMAS, G. and WITTS, M. M. The Destruction of San Francisco (Stein and
    Day 1971)

TWYNE, T. A Pithy Discourse of the Late Earthquake (1580)

WINTHROP, J. A Lecture on Earthquakes (1755)

WOODWARD, DR. J. The Natural History of the Earth (1726)

YOUNG, T. The History and Philosophy of Earthquakes (1757)

## Technical

BADGLEY, P. C. Structural and Tectonic Principles (Harper and Row 1965)

BATH, M. Introduction to Seismology (Wiley 1973)

BISHOP, R. E. D. Vibration (Cambridge University Press 1965)

COX, A. Plate Tectonics (Freeman 1973)

DAHLMAN, O. and ISRAELSON, H. Monitoring Underground Nuclear
    Explosions (Elsevier 1977)

DAVISON, C. Scales of Seismic Intensity (Bulletin, Seismological Society of
    America, Vol 11 and 23 1933)

DOWRICK, D. J. Earthquake Resistant Design (Wiley 1977)

HERSHBERGER, J. Intensity of Earthquake Accelerations with Intensity Ratings
    (Bulletin, Seismological Society of America Vol 46 1956)

JEFFREYS, H. The Earth (Cambridge University Press 1972)

LE PICHON, X. Plate Tectonics (Elsevier 1974)

MCKENZIE, D. P. The Nature of the Solid Earth (McGraw Hill 1972)

MELCHOIR, P. The Earth Tides (Pergamon Press 1966)

NEWMARK, N. M. and ROSENBLEUTH, E. Fundamentals of Earthquake
    Engineering (Prentice-Hall 1971)

RAYLEIGH, J. The Theory of Sound (Dover Publications 1945)
RICHTER, C. F. Elementary Seismology (Freeman 1958)
RIKITAKE, T. Earthquake Prediction (Elsevier 1975)
WIEGEL, R. L. Earthquake Engineering (Prentice-Hall 1970)
YANEV, P. Peace of Mind in Earthquake Country (Chronicle 1974)

# Picture Credits

Professor N. N. Ambraseys; British Library; British Museum; California Historical Society; Dartec Ltd.; International Tsunami Information Center, Honolulu, Hawaii; League of Red Cross Societies; the Mayor and Municipality of Skopje, Yugoslavia; National Aeronautics and Space Administration (NASA); National Earthquake Information Service (NEIS); National Oceanic and Atmospheric Administration/Environmental Data Service of the US Department of Commerce (NOAA/EDS); Novesti Press Agency; Radio Times Hulton Picture Library; Science Museum, London; Seismological Society of America; The Tate Gallery, London; US Department of the Interior, Geological Survey (USGS); Yasuda Fire and Marine Insurance Company, Tokyo.

Maps and Diagrams on pages 38, 52–3, 60, 61, 64, 66, 67, 200 and 207 by Eileen Batterberry.

# Index